Lessons in Licens

Microsoft 74-678: Exam Preparation Guide

By Louise Ulrick

Table of Contents

PART 1: INTRODUCTION

The Microsoft Certified Professional Certification

The Microsoft Certified Professional (MCP) is a certification that validates IT professional, developer, and licensing specialist expertise through industry-recognized exams. There is just one exam aimed at licensing professionals and passing this exam gives MCP status:

- 74-678: Designing and Providing Microsoft Volume Licensing Solutions to Large Organizations

Passing this MCP exam demonstrates that you have a good understanding of the Microsoft products and their licensing, and can ultimately recommend the right licensing solutions to a range of customers.

The MCP exams are also great if you're a Microsoft partner and want to differentiate yourself by acquiring some competencies through the Microsoft Partner Program. The Volume Licensing competency requires passes in this exam – two for the silver level, and four for the gold level, and the Software Asset Management competency requires two passes for the gold level.

If you're not a Microsoft partner but are instead someone who works for a customer organization and needs to know about Microsoft licensing, then this exam is great for you to test your knowledge and demonstrate that you know your stuff. In either circumstance, the certifications are valid world-wide and are great to have on your CV or résumé.

Exam 74-678 Syllabus

You can find the full list of the requirements for the exam at this link: https://www.microsoft.com/learning/en-us/exam-74-678.aspx.

However, in summary, the exam covers the four key areas below, and in Part 6 of this book we'll look in detail about what these mean and which sections will help you with the knowledge that you'll need:

- Recommend the appropriate technology solution
  (Determine the right on-premises or Online Services product to meet a customer's needs)

- Recommend the appropriate Software Assurance benefits
  (Determine the right SA benefits to meet a customer's needs)

- Recommend a licensing solution
  (Determine the right Volume Licensing program to meet a customer's needs)

- Provide post-sales customer service
  (Determine the right tools and resources for customers to access and activate software, and manage SA benefits)

Using this Book

The primary aim of this book is to help you to prepare for the 74-678 exam and, of course, to ultimately pass it. The book is designed to help you to pass the exam by teaching you the things that you need to know – it's not a list of all the exam questions that I and my many licensing acquaintances can remember from when we took the exam – you'll find plenty of resources on the Internet if that's the way you want to go! Learning the topics to pass the exam will also stand you in good stead in real life afterwards as well of course; the knowledge in this book is relevant and useful for when you need to advise any customers about licensing solutions.

I would recommend that you start at the beginning of this book and work your way through the sections in order. These sections cover all the topics that you'll need to know about in order to answer the exam questions based on the syllabus above, and give you lots of tips on how you should apply your knowledge in the exam. There are also summary tables throughout this book, and these are the things that you should try and learn for the exam.

At the end of each section you'll find some revision questions on the topics covered and you can choose how you use these; if you're pretty experienced with Microsoft licensing and you want to see how good your existing knowledge is, you could work through those questions and then read appropriate sections if you discover any particular weaknesses. You may want to do the questions as you work through the book, or you may want to do a big revision session when you've finished reading.

The final section consists of a sample scenario; this gives you a good flavor of the type of scenario that you can expect to find in the exam, and will help you to see if you've got any remaining gaps in your knowledge.

The exam is aimed at people who have at least six months' experience in Microsoft licensing; if you're new to Microsoft licensing it's probably worth doing some preparatory work outside of this book and I would recommend the Microsoft Get Licensing Ready certifications.

You can find the entry point to these certifications at the site www.getlicensingready.com and it's your choice as to how you work with the resources that you'll find there. There are over 20 modules in total that you can take an exam in, and each module has a video that explains all the concepts and a set of reference materials that form quick reference guides for those concepts. As a minimum (for new people) before you start working through this book, complete the first two modules that make up the Microsoft Licensing Solutions Specialist Lite certification.

And finally, throughout the explanations I've used the words "typically" and "generally". This is not me being imprecise so much as showing you how specific you need to be and what level of detail you need to know for the exam. If something disturbs you in my simplifications do email us at info@licensingschool.co.uk with suggestions to help make things clearer for others! You may also know other things about the licensing of the products that I haven't included – I've tried to keep to just the level of detail that is included in the exam, rather than attempting to create an exhaustive guide on the licensing of all the Microsoft products.

Product Versions

The exam that you will be taking was first made available in Se and the following products and versions are covered in the exa

- Windows 8.1
- Office 2013
- Windows Server 2012 R2
- System Center 2012 R2
- Project, Exchange, SharePoint, Lync 2013 versions
- SQL Server 2014
- Dynamics CRM Server 2013
- Windows Intune
- Office 365
- Enterprise Mobility Suite
- Microsoft Azure Services
- CRM Online

Note that there are always changes in Microsoft licensing, but any that have been implemented after September 2014 are not included in the exam, or in this book.

An Overview of the Exam

Although we take a more extensive look at the exam and the final preparation that you will want to do for it at the end of this book, I think it's worth having a quick overview here so that you know what you're aiming for as you work through the different sections.

The exam is closed-book and proctored. That is to say, you can't take any resources into the test room with you and it will be invigilated – either by a person in the room with you or via CCTV.

The exam has two sections: there will be a customer scenario and then a whole series of individual questions.

In the customer scenario you'll be given the background to the customer and told their current software situation, how they've acquired any current licenses, and their business goals. You'll be asked to recommend products, licenses, and then the programs to purchase those licenses through. You can expect to get around 10 – 12 questions on the scenario.

The individual questions section is composed of a whole range of questions on any aspect of licensing as defined in the syllabus above. Many of these will be multiple choice questions but there are also some new question types and you should make sure that you're familiar with these by working through Part 6 of this book. You can expect to get around 40 – 50 questions in this section.

You'll have up to 140 minutes to work through both the scenario and the questions and to pass, you'll need 700 points.

PART 2: THE MICROSOFT PRODUCTS AND THEIR LICENSING MODELS

For the exam, you need to be able to identify which product might meet a company's business needs, and be confident in selecting the right licensing model for that product. This section takes you through all the key products and how they're licensed, as well as giving you some tips as to how you should apply the knowledge in the exam.

If you already have a good knowledge of the Microsoft products and their licensing models, why not skip to the Recap Questions on page 88 and test yourself?

Some Fundamental Concepts

Before we leap into the world of the Microsoft products and their licensing, there are a couple of key concepts that we should cover first.

The first: what is a license? It's obviously a fundamental question! A Microsoft license gives a customer rights to use the software and we'll see throughout this book that the rights differ dependent on how they've purchased the software – either as a boxed product, pre-installed, or through a Volume Licensing program. All licenses give the customer the rights to install (where needed) and use the software, but additional rights, such as virtualization rights, are often only included when the licenses are purchased through a Volume Licensing program.

The second concept is the notion of versions and editions of Microsoft software – terms that I'll be using throughout this section. A version is a particular release of a piece of software and it often corresponds to a year – Office 2013, for example. An edition is a way of differentiating between different sets of functionality that are included in the product – Office Standard 2013 does not include as many components as Office Professional Plus 2013, for example.

Windows 8.1

Windows 8.1 is the Microsoft client operating system. This section of the book covers the general licensing of this product.

The Editions

Windows 8.1 is available in two editions for businesses – Windows 8.1 Pro and Windows 8.1 Enterprise. You should consider that Windows 8.1 Pro is the entry level product for businesses and then further features and functionality are included with the Enterprise edition.

There are three main features that you should recognize and associate with Windows 8.1 Enterprise edition:

- DirectAccess: enables users to work remotely without needing a VPN connection

- BranchCache: enables users in branch offices to quickly connect to information

- AppLocker: enables IT administrators to choose which applications can run

Don't get caught out by BitLocker: it was a feature of just the Enterprise edition in previous versions of Windows but for Windows 8.1 it is included in both the Pro and Enterprise editions.

Licensing Model

Windows 8.1 is licensed by device: a license is assigned to a device and the software is licensed to be used on that device.

Availability

As you know, the exam focuses on recommending licensing solutions for large organizations and this will primarily be through Volume Licensing agreements. However, Windows is often acquired pre-installed and so you need to know what editions are available through the OEM and Volume Licensing channels. Essentially, Windows 8.1 Pro is available through both channels, and Windows 8.1 Enterprise is only available through the Volume Licensing programs.

License Types

There are two types of Windows licenses: full licenses and upgrade licenses. When you buy Windows pre-installed on a new computer through the OEM channel it's a full license that is assigned to the device.

Windows licenses that are purchased through Volume Licensing programs are upgrade licenses only, which means that they can only be assigned to a device that has a qualifying underlying operating system. The qualifying operating system must be a business operating system, so Windows 8 or Windows 7 Home Premium editions would not qualify, for example.

Software Assurance

There's a whole section on Software Assurance in this book and you'll probably have come across the concept before. SA can be added to a Windows license for an organization to gain access to an additional set of use rights. The licensing rules were changed with Windows 8.1 and today Software Assurance may only be added to the Enterprise edition. This does mean that if an organization purchases their Windows licenses through the OEM channel they can no longer add SA to them since it's only the Pro licenses that are available through this channel.

License Reassignment Rights

Typically there are restrictions on how often a device license may be moved between different devices; Windows 8.1 Pro licenses acquired through either the OEM channel or through Volume Licensing may not be moved.

If Software Assurance has been added to a Windows 8.1 Enterprise Upgrade license then it may be moved to another device while the SA coverage is active.

Downgrade and Down Edition Rights

One of the benefits of acquiring licenses through a Volume Licensing program is the availability of downgrade rights. However, OEM licenses do give some downgrade rights as the table below shows. Typically, this right is to the last two versions of the product, but note the slight anomaly in that the previous version of Windows 8.1 Pro is considered to be Windows 7 Professional rather than Windows 8 Pro.

Windows 8.1 Enterprise also gives Down Edition rights – not only can you install an earlier version of the same edition (Windows 7 Enterprise, for example) but you can also install different editions – Windows 8 Pro or Windows Vista Business, for example. Not all products have down edition rights so you shouldn't assume that they do, and I'll point out the products that they do apply to as we go through this section of the book.

	Windows 8.1 Pro (OEM)	Windows 8.1 Pro (VL Upgrade)	Windows 8.1 Enterprise (VL Upgrade)
Windows 8 Enterprise			✓
Windows 8 Pro		✓	✓
Windows 7 Enterprise			✓
Windows 7 Professional	✓	✓	✓
Windows Vista Enterprise			✓
Windows Vista Business	✓	✓	✓
Windows XP Professional		✓	✓
Windows 2000 Professional		✓	✓
Windows 95/98/NT		✓	✓

Figure 1: Windows 8.1 Downgrade and Down Edition Rights

Applying your knowledge in the exam:

- Look for business goals that state that the organization needs a high level of functionality in their client operating system since this would drive a requirement for the Enterprise edition of Windows 8.1. Make sure that you learn the three features specific to the Enterprise edition

- If you are asked to recommend the number of licenses required for a Windows 8.1 deployment where you're given the number of users and devices, remember that Windows is licensed by device so you should count the devices for the number of required licenses

- Remember that Windows 8.1 Pro or Enterprise licenses acquired through Volume Licensing programs are Upgrade licenses which require an underlying qualifying operating system license. Be prepared to pick out any operating systems that wouldn't qualify by looking for those with the word "Home" in the edition name

- You may be asked to recommend a method for purchasing Windows 8.1 licenses. If the customer is buying new hardware and needs only Windows 8.1 Pro then recommend that Windows is purchased through OEM

- If you identify that a customer has a need for Software Assurance on their Windows licenses then you need to recommend the Enterprise edition which can only be acquired through the Volume Licensing programs

- If a customer scenario involves reassigning Windows licenses, remember that this is only allowed when there is active SA on the license to be moved

- Remember that there ARE downgrade rights for Windows acquired through the OEM channel – this is the only product for which there are

- Look out for business goals that state that there is a need to standardize on a particular version and edition of Windows; you should recommend that the customer acquires Windows through a Volume Licensing agreement since this will give them the most flexibility in both downgrade and down edition rights

Office 2013

Office 2013 is the Microsoft suite of desktop productivity tools and is a cost-effective way for organizations to license all of these products.

The Office Products

The Office suite products are the following products:

- Word 2013: a word-processing tool
- Excel 2013: a spreadsheet tool
- PowerPoint 2013: a graphics and presentation tool
- Outlook 2013: the email client with calendar, tasks and contacts functionality
- OneNote 2013: a note-taking and information gathering application
- Publisher 2013: a desktop publishing tool
- Access 2013: the end user database solution
- Lync 2013: the client application for the Lync Server product
- InfoPath 2013: an application for building and consuming electronic forms

In addition, there are two Office-branded products that are also available as separate purchases:

- Visio 2013: an Office family product for creating sophisticated diagrams
- Project 2013: an Office family product for creating project plans

The Editions and Availability

Office 2013 is available in a number of different editions, and the availability of these differs by the channel that Office is purchased through. For instance, there are two business editions of Office available through the Volume Licensing programs – Standard and Professional Plus, and just one edition through OEM and FPP – Professional. You may hear the term "PKC" in association with Office acquired through the OEM and FPP channel – this stands for Product Key Card and refers to the key that will activate the software.

The diagram below shows which products are in which editions. For many years, the difference between Office Standard and Office Professional was Access, and this is still the case. "Ali" will help you to remember the extra products that are in Office Professional Plus 2013 over Standard: Access, Lync, and InfoPath (the initial letters of these products spell out the name Ali!)

	Office Standard 2013	Office Professional 2013	Office Professional Plus 2013
Word 2013	✔	✔	✔
Excel 2013	✔	✔	✔
PowerPoint 2013	✔	✔	✔
Outlook 2013	✔	✔	✔
OneNote 2013	✔	✔	✔
Publisher 2013	✔	✔	✔
Access 2013		✔	✔
Lync 2013			✔
InfoPath 2013			✔

Figure 2: Editions of Office 2013

Licensing Model
Office 2013 is licensed by device: a license is assigned to a device and the software is licensed to be used on that device.

License Types

Office licenses acquired through any channel are full licenses, and are a special type of license called a Suite license. This means that a license is assigned to a device and then all of the Office products must be installed on that single device rather than being split across a number of devices.

Software Assurance

Software Assurance may be added to Office 2013 licenses acquired through a Volume Licensing program or OEM. If the licenses have been acquired through a Volume Licensing program then it must be added at the time of purchase, and if Office has been purchased pre-installed then it must be added within 90 days of the purchase of the device. Note that Software Assurance can only be purchased through a Volume Licensing program so an organization would need to have an active agreement to make SA purchases through.

There's one other quirk that you need to know about SA. When you add SA to an OEM Office Professional license you actually add Office Standard SA within the Volume Licensing program.

License Reassignment Rights

Office licenses that are purchased through the OEM channel may never be reassigned to another device – they live and die on the machine with which they were purchased. Office licenses acquired through the Volume Licensing programs may be assigned to another device – as long as it is no more frequently than every 90 days.

Downgrade and Down Edition Rights

Downgrade rights for Office are only available if you purchase licenses through the Volume Licensing channel. So if a customer buys a license for Office Professional Plus 2013 then they can install Office Professional Plus 2010 if that suits their business better. Note however that there are NO down edition rights for Office, even when it's purchased through Volume Licensing. This means that a license for Office Professional Plus 2013 does NOT permit you to install Office Standard 2013 in its place.

Portable Use Rights

When Office is acquired through some Volume Licensing programs then portable use rights for Office are available; if a customer has purchased an Office license for a device, then he is also allowed to install Office on a second portable device for the exclusive use of the main user of the originally licensed device. Note that this is not a way to reduce the licenses required in all situations; customers wouldn't be compliant, for example, if they used portable use rights to license the use of Office on a portable device for a second user. Note also that where there is a requirement within a Volume Licensing program to license all devices in an organization, these rights are not available.

Network Usage Rights

Another right that is granted when an Office license is acquired through a Volume Licensing program is the right to install Office on a server and use it from there. This means that in RDS and VDI scenarios (see the following sections for more details) an Office license is assigned to each device that will access Office but the right to install Office on the server and access it there is included in the license rights. This right is not part of an Office OEM or FPP license.

Enhanced Server Integration

When you buy Office licenses through the Volume Licensing programs the products have an enhanced connection to backend servers. This enables scenarios such as Information Rights Management (IRM) through Windows Server 2012 R2, Enterprise Content Management (ECM) through SharePoint Server 2013, and access to sophisticated email archiving through Exchange Server 2013.

Applying your knowledge in the exam:

- Remember that Office is licensed by device, so when you're asked to recommend the required number of licenses in a particular situation, it's the number of devices that the products will be used on that is important, not the number of users using them

- Although Office licenses purchased through a Volume Licensing program can be reassigned to a different device, don't forget the 90 day rule. In the exam, don't be misled by scenarios where ten users use ten of the twenty machines one day, and a different ten machines the next day and so on – the licenses can't follow the users around in this way, and you would need to ensure that all of the machines were licensed

- Make sure that you're familiar with the one-liner descriptions of the Office products above so that you can confidently answer questions where you're told that a company needs a tool for its users to give them certain functionality and you need to choose the most appropriate product

- Make sure that you're familiar with the products in the key Office editions mentioned above; you could be given a scenario with a list of products that are required and you need to be able to recommend the correct edition of Office to meet these business goals

- Equally, make sure you know which editions are available through which channel – if you're asked to recommend how customers should acquire some Office Professional Plus 2013 licenses there is no choice – it's just through the Volume Licensing programs

- Don't forget that Visio and Project, although Office branded, are not part of the Office suites themselves, so a customer licensed for Office Professional Plus 2013 would need to make additional license purchases if they wanted to use either of these products

- Remember that the Office components can't be split between machines, so when you're asked to count up the number of licenses required, make sure that you take this into account

- On the same note, remember that portable use rights can't be allocated to more than one user. So if the scenario you're given details that five people use a desktop machine and another five people use portable devices, you would need to recommend ten licenses since there are ten different individuals using Office on the ten devices

- If a customer scenario involves running Office from a server in either an RDS or VDI environment, don't forget that this right is only part of the Volume Licensing license

- If you're asked to state which downgrade rights are available to a particular customer, remember that it's vital that you know how the licenses were acquired – downgrade rights are only available through a Volume Licensing program and there are NO down edition rights through any channel

- If the customer scenario involves attaching SA to an Office license, remember that it must be done at point of purchase if it's a Volume Licensing license whereas a customer has 90 days to attach it to an OEM license where Office Standard 2013 SA may be attached to Office Professional 2013

- And, finally, remember the more sophisticated links to the backend servers that are built into the Volume Licensing editions of Office as it could be another factor that is mentioned as a customer is deciding to acquire Office licenses

Virtual Desktop Infrastructure

So far we've covered the licensing of Windows and Office in a physical infrastructure – in other words, the products were installed directly onto client devices. As an alternative, an organization may want to set up virtual desktops on their servers and to have their users access them from their desktop machines – a setup known as a Virtual Desktop Infrastructure (VDI).

The diagram below shows a server at Spring Green Grocers' head office running personalized Windows Enterprise 8.1 and Office Professional Plus 2013 desktops that are being delivered to the end user desktop machines:

Figure 3: Virtual Desktop Infrastructure

Although the desktop machines do not have Windows and Office installed on them, they do still need to be licensed for both Windows and Office. The licensing changes dependent on the particular scenario and we'll cover these scenarios in the next few pages. Users do need to be licensed for server access too and we'll look at that in the final part.

Licensing VDI for Corporate-owned x86 Devices
The first scenario we'll take is one where Spring Green Grocers want to license corporate-owned x86 devices for VDI desktops. Consider an x86 device to be a device like a PC or a Mac rather than an iPad which doesn't run a full version of Windows.

As we've said, these devices will be running Windows and Office in the VDI infrastructure and so need to be licensed for both of these products. I think it's easiest to start by taking the licensing of each in turn.

An ordinary Windows 8.1 Enterprise license purchased through a Volume Licensing agreement allows the installation of Windows on the physical desktop device – it's only when you add SA that you get the added deployment flexibility of being allowed to create, store and run virtual desktops on a server. So, a Windows license is assigned to the device and SA is added.

An Office license is also assigned to the device and, actually, that's all you need for this scenario. If you refer back to the Network Usage Rights section on page 16 you may remember that an Office license acquired through a Volume Licensing program gives the rights to install Office on a server and use it from there – which is what we're doing in this scenario.

So, in summary, both Windows and Office licenses need to be assigned to the device that is running the VDI desktop, and the Windows license needs to have SA too. If we just take Mrs. Lime in the diagram above, this is what it looks like, and she's allowed to take that machine wherever she likes and access her VDI desktop. You can see that there's an asset tag assigned to her machine indicating that it's corporate-owned:

Figure 4: VDI Licensing – Corporate-owned x86 Device

Licensing VDI for Third Party-owned Devices used Off-Premises

Let's stay with Mrs. Lime: she has a corporate-owned primary device licensed for VDI with Windows SA and Office and we know that she can take that device anywhere she wants and access her VDI desktop from it.

However, in this scenario she goes home and she wants to access her VDI desktop from her personally-owned desktop machine. How's this licensed? Well, following the usual rules, we know that the machine needs to be licensed for Windows and Office but consider how expensive this is going to be if she then wants to access the VDI desktop from her iPad as well. However, because she is the primary user of a device licensed with Windows with SA and Office there's a cost-effective way of licensing this scenario.

The solution is Roaming Use Rights which are an SA benefit for both Windows and Office. Roaming Use Rights relax the licensing rules completely and as long as three key conditions are met, allow users to access their VDI desktops on third party-owned devices outside of the corporate premises, which is just what we want in this case.

The conditions are "who", "what" and "where". The "who" must be the primary user of a device licensed with both Windows and Office with SA. The "what" is the device – it must be third party-owned, and the "where" specifies that the device must be used outside of the corporate premises.

Mrs. Lime is indeed the primary user of a device with Windows with SA and Office so if we make sure that SA is acquired with the Office license then she qualifies as the primary user of a correctly licensed device. Note that a primary user is just defined as the person who uses the device for more than 50% of the time. The other two conditions are met too – she owns the device, not Spring Green Grocers, and she's at home so she's definitely not on the corporate premises.

Licensing VDI for Corporate-owned non-x86 Primary Devices

Let's now extend our scenario for Spring Green Grocers and welcome Mrs. Periwinkle. Mrs. Periwinkle works on a part-time basis and has been assigned a corporate-owned iPad from which she needs to access her VDI desktop.

So, how's this licensed? Well, the same principles apply – the iPad needs to be licensed for Windows and Office in the same way that Mrs. Lime's laptop was. However, in this case we can't assign an ordinary Windows 8.1 Enterprise Upgrade license with SA because this license requires that there's a qualifying underlying operating system – and the iPad can't run Windows so it won't have this license.

In this case you assign a different license for the Windows portion, and the license that's needed is the Windows Virtual Desktop Access license. For the purposes of the exam, you should consider this license to be exactly equivalent to a Windows 8.1 Enterprise license with SA, with just two important differences: there is no qualifying operating system required, and it doesn't give any local installation rights.

There are no restrictions on assigning an Office license to an iPad so here are the licenses required for Mrs. Periwinkle in this scenario and, again, she's allowed to use this device wherever she likes:

Figure 5: VDI Licensing – Corporate-owned non-x86 Device

Licensing VDI for Corporate-owned non-x86 Companion Devices

Mr. Orange is our next user to consider and he's been given a corporate-owned iPad as a secondary device from which he needs to access his VDI desktop. He already has a primary device which is a laptop which has been licensed correctly for VDI with a Windows with SA license, and an Office license. Because he has a fully licensed primary device, then this secondary non-x86 device becomes a companion device and there is a cost-effective way of licensing this for Windows.

The primary device is licensed for Windows 8.1 Enterprise with SA and thus becomes eligible to have a Windows Companion Subscription License (CSL) assigned to it. What this license does is enable the primary user of the device to which it's been assigned to access the Windows portion of their VDI desktop on a corporate-owned non-x86 device. (It actually allows more than just that, but let's stick with our example for the moment!)

So the iPad doesn't need to be licensed for Windows since it's covered by this CSL license, it just needs an Office license assigned to it and Mr. Orange is all set to go. Again, he can use his VDI desktop on this device wherever he wants:

Figure 6: VDI Licensing – Corporate-owned non-x86 Companion Device

Note that an alternative way of licensing this scenario would be to purchase VDA licenses for any further devices, but the Companion Subscription License is a more cost-effective option, so recommend that if you can.

Licensing VDI for Third Party-owned Devices used On-Premises

For this last scenario we'll stay with Mr. Orange. In the time since he's been given a corporate-owned iPad he's bought himself another tablet device and on occasions he feels it would be convenient to access his VDI desktop from that – either when he's at home or in the office.

This is the other use for the Companion Subscription License – to license Windows on third party-owned devices which can be used anywhere. The CSL licenses up to 5 devices for Windows so Mr. Orange is well within this limit as he just has a corporate-owned iPad and a personally-owned tablet that he wants to cover.

But what about the Office license? Again, the tablet would need to be licensed for Office and you can imagine that with several devices needing Office licenses it's going to get expensive. So, the best way to license this scenario would actually be to buy Mr. Orange an Office 365 ProPlus USL which licenses him for use of Office on up to 5 devices. Thus, the best way to license this scenario is shown below, where the little house symbol indicates it's a personally owned device:

Figure 7: VDI Licensing – Third Party-owned Devices used On-Premises

Server Licensing Requirements

The final part of the VDI story is to consider what CALs are required to access the VDI desktops on the server. Since you're preparing for a Microsoft exam it would make sense to assume that the VDI server is a Microsoft one and, in that case, it's Windows Server 2012 R2 and Remote Desktop Services that need to be licensed. There's detail in the Windows Server 2012 R2 section of this book but it's quite straightforward – each user or device needs a Windows Server 2012 CAL and an RDS 2012 CAL. Of course in the scenarios where a user has multiple devices it would make sense to have User CALs.

Applying your knowledge in the exam:

- I've been very accurate in the licensing above. For the exam, you should assume that a device will have Windows AND Office SA so the primary user will be covered to use that device inside and outside of the corporate premises, as well as to access their VDI desktop on any third party-owned device outside of the office. Don't forget to include the Windows Server and RDS CALs in your licensing recommendations too

- Remember that the VDA license is an alternative to Windows + SA when there is no qualifying operating system on a device so look out for the types of devices that users will use – if there are iPads or other non-Windows tablets then a VDA license is likely to be the right recommendation

- Remember the two key scenarios when a Windows Companion Subscription License is useful – when a primary user is assigned a secondary, non x-86 device, or when he wants to bring any sort of personal device into the corporate premises and access his VDI desktop there. This will only license the Windows part of the desktop so remember that Office licenses will still be required per device and that an Office 365 ProPlus USL could be a good alternative

Windows Server 2012 R2

Windows Server 2012 R2 is the Microsoft server operating system product and there are two editions aimed at larger customers: Standard and Datacenter editions. You need to know how these editions are licensed and to be able to work out how many licenses are required for a given server, and you also need to be able to calculate the licenses needed in a virtualized infrastructure. You do need to be able to recommend an edition of Windows Server 2012 R2 based on a customer's requirements, but these days the editions have the same functionality and your recommendation will be based on how heavily they want to virtualize their infrastructure since it's just virtualization rights that distinguish the two editions.

Licensing Windows Server 2012 R2

Windows Server 2012 R2 is licensed with the Processor-based and CAL model. Licenses are assigned to a server based on the number of physical processors in that server, with one license covering up to two processors. So a single processor machine would need one license assigned to it, and a server with four processors would need two licenses. All processors in the server must always be licensed.

Then, any clients accessing the services of the server need to be licensed with a Client Access License – a CAL, as shown in the following diagram:

Figure 8: Processor-based and CAL Licensing

CALs almost always come in two types – a User CAL or a Device CAL, and both are available for Windows Server 2012 R2.

Organizations buy User CALs when a single user will use multiple devices to access the services of the server. The CAL is assigned to the user, and that user may use any device to access the services of the server as shown in the diagram below:

Figure 9: User CAL

Organizations buy Device CALs when a single device will be used by many users to access the services of the server. The CAL is assigned to a device, and any user may use that device to access the services of the server as shown in the diagram below:

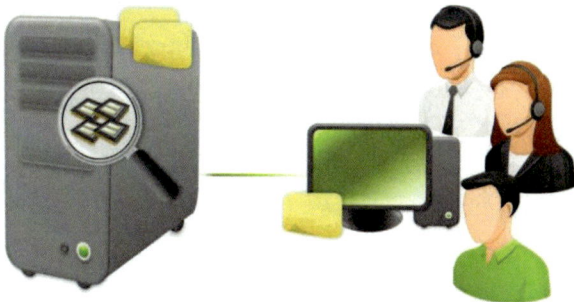

Figure 10: Device CAL

Organizations can generally mix and match these CALs if required, but it does become more difficult to ensure compliance.

Once users or devices have been assigned CALs they may access any of the servers on the network; for example, if an organization has purchased Windows Server CALs for all users, then those users may access any Windows Server on the network. The caveat to this is that the version of the CAL must be the same or higher than the version of the server. In other words, a Windows Server 2012 CAL may access a Windows 2012 server AND/OR a Windows 2008 server, but a Windows Server 2008 CAL may only access a Windows 2008 server, not a Windows 2012 server. Note that the latest edition of Windows Server is 2012 R2 but the corresponding CAL is 2012.

Licensing Virtualized Environments

Technology within Windows Server called Hyper-V enables customers to create and manage virtual machines on their physical servers, allowing them to consolidate servers and to gain some ease of manageability.

Let's take a look at how the licensing for Windows Server 2012 R2 works in a virtualized environment by considering a server with four processors on which six virtual machines need to be run. We know that the physical processors must always be licensed so, starting with the Datacenter edition, we would need to assign 2 licenses to this device (one license for every two processors). Having assigned the licenses to the machine the customer then receives rights to run a certain number of virtual machines, and in the case of the Datacenter edition, it's an unlimited number.

The diagram below shows the server licensed with Datacenter edition licenses and then the six virtual machines running:

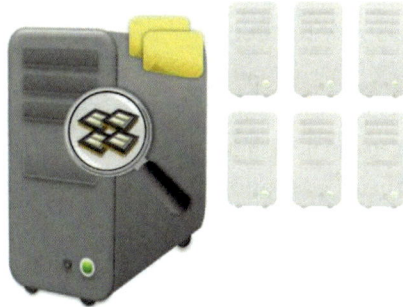

Figure 11: Licensing Virtual Machines with Windows Server 2012 R2 Datacenter

The licensing of Standard edition in a virtualized environment works in exactly the same way but the number of virtual machines that you're allowed to run is less. If we consider the same physical server with its four processors we'd again assign 2 licenses, but for Standard edition we only get rights to run two virtual machines per license. In this case we need to run six virtual machines and so you "stack" licenses – in other words, assign additional licenses to the server to receive rights to run additional virtual machines. As the diagram below shows, you'd need to assign 3 Standard licenses to the server to run the six virtual machines:

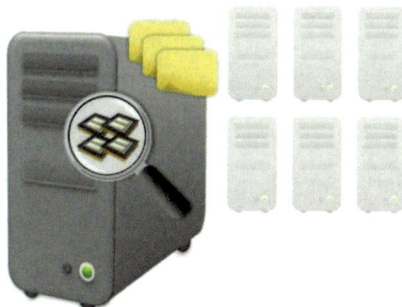

Figure 12: Licensing Virtual Machines with Windows Server 2012 R2 Standard

So how do you decide between using Standard and Datacenter licenses? From a cost perspective, Standard licenses are about 15% of the price of a Datacenter license and there's a break-even point when it's more cost-effective to assign Datacenter licenses rather than Standard licenses, and that's at about seven virtual machines for every two processors. However, it's much easier to ensure compliance if you license with Datacenter edition since you can run an unlimited number of virtual machines without having to worry about specifically assigning additional licenses as additional virtual machines are added to the infrastructure. In real life, customers will weigh up the costs against the convenience in the context of their future plans for their server farms.

For the exam, if a customer will only lightly virtualize their infrastructure – say run ten virtual machines or less on an individual server – then Windows Server 2012 R2 Standard edition will be the right recommendation for them, otherwise, above that, they should use Datacenter edition. Don't try to read too much into the exam questions – if you're being given the steer that virtualization is key, then take that as a hint that you should be recommending Datacenter edition.

Licensing External Users

An organization licensing a server infrastructure will license its servers and its users and then potentially needs to license its external users. There are official definitions of what constitutes an external user, but for the purposes of the exam consider that these users are people who aren't employees of the organization but do need to access the system.

For products licensed with CALs, the organization could always choose to buy CALs for its external users, but it's generally more cost-effective, and easier to manage, to buy an External Connector license, since an External Connector license is a single license that allows an unlimited number of external users to access a server. An External Connector license is an Additive license – in other words, it can never be purchased alone, it needs to be purchased in conjunction with the underlying server license. For Windows Server 2012 R2 there is a single External Connector license that is applied to a server device regardless of which edition of Windows Server 2012 R2 is powering that server. Note that, like the CALs, there is no R2 version of the External Connector license, so the current version of this license is the Windows Server 2012 External Connector.

The diagram below shows a network infrastructure with three servers, all of which have two Windows Server licenses assigned to them. The shaded server at the top also has an External Connector license assigned to it allowing any number of external users to access it:

Figure 13: External Connector License

Applying your knowledge in the exam:

- Look out for business goals that specify how many devices users will use; if they are using multiple devices you are likely to recommend User CALs, whereas if they are sharing devices, recommend Device CALs

- Look out for business goals that indicate that users will be working from home. In most cases, this will lead you to recommend User CALs so that users are licensed both at their work devices and their home machines

- Look out for business goals that state that an organization needs to give access to its external users. Although they do have the choice of assigning CALs to these users, in almost all cases it is going to be more cost-effective to buy an External Connector license and that should be in your mind as your first recommendation

- Remember that External Connector licenses need to be applied to individual servers so if the customer's current situation or future plans involve allowing external users to access their multi-server infrastructure, you would need to recommend an External Connector license for each server

- Make sure that you're comfortable with calculating the licenses required for a given server in a physical environment

- Remember that there are no separate licensing requirements for Hyper-V; it's just technology included in Windows Server that allows customers to set up and manage virtual machines

- When you're calculating the licenses required in a virtual infrastructure remember that the physical server needs to be fully licensed regardless of how many virtual machines are running

- Do make sure that you can calculate the licenses required in a virtual infrastructure where Standard licenses have been used and you may need to stack the licenses on the physical server

- If you're told that a customer is intending to heavily virtualize his server farm then take this as a steer to recommend the Datacenter edition, since the only difference between Standard and Datacenter editions are the virtualization rights

Windows Server 2012 R2 Services

Windows Server 2012 R2 includes two important services that you need to know about for the exam: Remote Desktop Services and Rights Management Services.

Remote Desktop Services

Remote Desktop Services was previously known as Terminal Services and very often in real life (and certainly for the purposes of the exam) it allows an organization to install Office on a server and to have users access it from their client devices over the network. All of the application processing is done on the server, and it's been a great way for organizations to continue to use older hardware since the client device does not need to be powerful enough to run Office.

There are some important licensing concepts to be aware of in the licensing of Remote Desktop Services and we're going to take the example of running Office on the server, as it's the one you're most likely to come across in the exam. For this scenario, from a server perspective, the server needs to be licensed with a Windows Server license – there are no other licensing requirements for the RDS component on the server. Then, all of the client devices need to be licensed with Windows CALs and, in addition, if they're using the services of RDS (which they are in our scenario) with RDS CALs too. Since Office will be used on the client devices, there needs to be an Office license assigned to the device too. Office will actually be installed and running on the server and there's just one licensing requirement associated with this – that the Office license has to be purchased through a Volume Licensing agreement. As we saw before, acquiring Office through Volume Licensing gives Network Usage Rights which allows an organization to install the software on a server and have the client devices access it remotely. Note that you don't need an extra license to install Office on the server; if you've got 350 PCs accessing the copy on the server you simply need 350 VL licenses for the devices.

There is an External Connector available to license RDS for external users.

Active Directory Rights Management Services

AD RMS can be used to protect documents using information rights management (IRM) which allows a user to attach access permissions to a particular document which can prevent it from being printed, forwarded or copied by unauthorized people, for example.

In common with RDS, there are no additional licensing requirements on the Windows Server itself, but every user or device that access the AD RMS services of the server must be covered with an AD RMS CAL.

Again, for external users there is an AD RMS External Connector available.

Applying your knowledge in the exam:

- The business goals may state quite specifically that the organization wants to use Office applications with RDS, or may describe a need for users to access Office remotely. Make sure that you don't fall into the trap of recommending that they acquire their Office licenses through OEM, since OEM licenses don't include the required remote access rights. Also ensure that you recommend a Volume Licensing Office license for each of the devices that will access Office on the server

- Although RDS is a service of Windows Server, remember that it is licensed with CALs, so don't forget to include both Windows Server and RDS CALs when recommending licenses in an RDS scenario

- Likewise, although there are no additional server licensing requirements when utilizing IRM, remember to include both Windows Server and AD RMS CALs in your licensing recommendations

- The components of the Core and Enterprise CAL Suites are listed on page 50 and you'll see that the AD RMS CAL is included as part of the Enterprise CAL Suite. Therefore, if you're recommending what licenses a customer needs to license an IRM solution check whether or not they already have this license

System Center 2012 R2

The Microsoft products that enable organizations to manage their client and server infrastructure are all part of the System Center family. Historically, there have been a number of different products for different management tasks, but with System Center 2012 these were consolidated into a single product with eight components.

System Center Licensing Model

The System Center licensing model is shown in the diagram below. The large server represents the management server where the System Center management product is installed, and every device that is managed by that server needs to have either a Client or a Server Management License assigned to it. Note that although software is installed on the management server there is no requirement to license it – the rights to install the software here are included in the Management Licenses. Likewise, SQL Server is required to support the management server, and rights to install that are also included:

Figure 14: System Center 2012 R2 Licensing

Licensing System Center 2012 R2 for Servers

The Server Management Licenses (MLs) are assigned to the server devices following the same Processor-based licensing model as Windows Server 2012 R2. As a reminder, one System Center 2012 R2 license covers up to two processors in the physical server and thus you can see just one license assigned to each of the managed servers in Figure 14.

In common with Windows Server 2012 R2 there are two editions of System Center 2012 R2 – Standard and Datacenter edition – and again it's just the virtualization rights that differ between them.

Licensing Virtualized Server Environments

The rules for licensing servers in a virtualized environment are exactly the same as for Windows Server 2012 R2 but let's have a look at an example specifically for System Center 2012 R2. In the diagram below, there's a physical server running four virtual machines with various workloads which we want to license so that each of the virtual machines may be managed by System Center 2012 R2. You can see that two licenses have been assigned to the physical server and this would make the server compliant both for the Standard and Datacenter editions:

Figure 15: System Center 2012 R2 Virtualization Licensing

As a reminder, when you license the physical server completely as we have done in the example above, you receive rights to manage a certain number of virtual machines. With the Datacenter edition it's an unlimited number, and with Standard edition it's two virtual machines per license. So, what would happen if we needed to add another two virtual machines to the physical server to be managed? If the two licenses in the diagram are Datacenter licenses then any additional virtual machines are already covered and if they are Standard licenses, then another license would need to be assigned to the physical server.

Core Infrastructure Server Suites

It's worth covering the Core Infrastructure Server Suites at this point. These suites are available in Standard and Datacenter editions and are a way of buying licenses for both Windows Server 2012 R2 and System Center 2012 R2. As you can imagine, the CIS Standard Suite includes the Standard edition of Windows Server and System Center, and CIS Datacenter includes the Datacenter edition of both products. The Suites follow the same licensing rules as the individual products with one Processor-based license covering up to two processors in a physical server, and with the same virtualization rules that we've already discussed.

As you might expect, buying the products together as a Suite attracts a discount when they're purchased through the Volume Licensing programs, the largest of which is available when they are purchased with an Enterprise-Wide Commitment through the Server and Cloud Enrollment and we'll look at the specific details for that in Part 3 of this book.

Licensing System Center 2012 R2 for Clients

Client Management Licenses (CMLs) must be purchased for any client devices managed by System Center 2012 R2 but these are split into three different offerings rather than the single "System Center 2012 R2" license for the servers:

- System Center 2012 R2 Configuration Manager CML
- System Center 2012 R2 Endpoint Protection SL
- System Center 2012 R2 Client Management Suite CML

Many customers will acquire these licenses through the CAL Suites and the Core CAL Suite includes the first two licenses, and the Enterprise CAL Suite includes all of them. Certainly for the purposes of the exam you should consider that customers will buy the CAL Suites rather than the individual components.

Applying your knowledge in the exam:

- Remember that although management software and SQL Server are required and installed on the management server, there are no licensing requirements for this server since the rights to both of these products are included in the Management Licenses. Hence any licensing recommendations you make should take account of this

- Be prepared to calculate the System Center 2012 R2 licenses required for a server in both physical and virtual environments

- You may need to recommend the right edition of System Center 2012 R2 – Standard or Datacenter – and remember that it's the virtualization rights that differ between the two editions. So, if the customer's environment is hinting at heavy virtualization then recommend the Datacenter edition

- Remember that the Core CAL Suite has the System Center Configuration Manager (SCCM) CML included in it. This is important when you're recommending licenses for an organization and you know they need to license SCCM for client machines but you can't see the CMLs called out specifically in the answer choices. Look instead for a choice with the Core CAL Suite. Equally, if it appears that the organization wants to deploy all of the System Center products, then look for the Enterprise CAL Suite as an answer as it contains all of the Client Management Licenses for the System Center products

- If you're asked to recommend how a customer should acquire their System Center 2012 R2 licenses, don't forget to check whether they also have a requirement for Windows Server 2012 R2, since this would lead you to recommend acquiring licenses through the Core Infrastructure Server Suites

Project Server 2013

Project Server 2013 is a project management server solution that allows project managers, key stakeholders, and other team members to collaborate on a project. The project plans themselves are created in Project Professional 2013 by a project manager and then saved to the Project Server. It's quite likely that no one else on the project will then use Project Professional, they'll just use a web browser to connect to the server to either see what tasks they've been assigned (as a team member) or to see whether the project is progressing to time and budget (as a key stakeholder).

Licensing Project Server 2013

Project Server 2013 is licensed with the Server / CAL licensing model. In this model there's a Project Server 2013 license assigned to the server and then users or devices are licensed with Project Server 2013 CALs, as shown in the diagram below. All users, whether they are accessing Project Server 2013 from a browser or Project Professional, must be licensed with a CAL.

Figure 16: Project Server 2013 Licensing

There's a special exception for customers who purchase Project Professional 2013 – they are deemed to have one Project Server 2013 Device CAL, so do bear that in mind when you are making licensing recommendations.

Licensing Virtualized Environments

A Project Server license is assigned to a physical server and then allows the software to be run in either the physical operating system environment or a single virtual machine. Extra licenses can be assigned to a physical server to allow Project Server to run in multiple virtual machines.

Licensing External Users

There is no External Connector license available for Project Server 2013, so an organization must buy Project Server CALs for its external users to access the services of their Project Servers.

Required Infrastructure Products

There are two products that are required pieces of the technology infrastructure for Project Server: SQL Server and SharePoint Server, and so any licensing recommendations you make for Project Server should also include licenses for these products. From a SQL Server perspective, this can be covered with either Core licenses or Server and CALs, and for SharePoint, both Standard and Enterprise CALs are required.

Note that if external users are being licensed they need to be licensed for these products too, and don't forget the Windows Server element either which is likely to be covered by an External Connector license.

Applying your knowledge in the exam:

- Remember to include CALs in your licensing recommendations for users who access Project Server 2013 through their browsers

- Remember that there is a single CAL for Project Server 2013 and don't be misled if you have to choose the relevant CALs and you see some fictional Project Standard and Enterprise CALs

- Many products now license external users via the Server license but Project is not one so make sure that you include Project Server CALs in any licensing recommendations for external users

- Learn the required infrastructure products for Project Server 2013 and make sure you include them in your licensing recommendations

Exchange Server 2013

Exchange Server 2013 is the Microsoft email server. Users can access their email, as well as calendar and contact information from Outlook, from the Outlook Web App, or from a mobile device through a variety of apps.

Licensing Exchange Server 2013

Exchange Server 2013 is licensed with the Server / CAL model but rather than there just being one level of CAL available, there are two CALs available for organizations to purchase. These CALs allow access to different levels of functionality, which means that customers can be licensed for whatever functionality their users need to use.

The two CALs are Standard and Enterprise CALs. The Standard CALs are often known as Base CALs and the Enterprise CALs as Additive CALs. An Additive CAL may only ever be purchased in addition to a Base CAL, never solely alone. This means that customers must purchase Standard CALs for all users accessing an Exchange Server and then, additionally, Enterprise CALs for those users who need access to the higher level functionality.

The diagram below shows some users licensed with just Standard CALs, and others licensed with both Standard and Enterprise CALs. The Standard CAL and the functionality that this allows the user or device to access on the server is shown in the darker color, and the Enterprise CAL and corresponding functionality is shown in the lighter color:

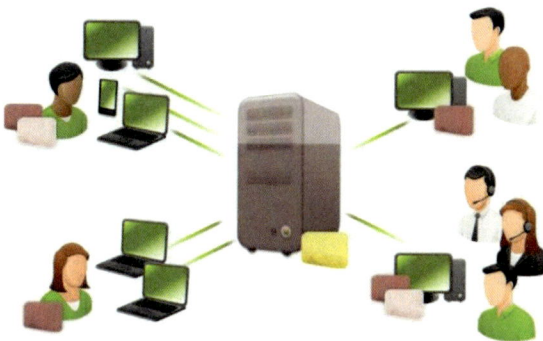

Figure 17: Exchange Server 2013 Licensing

Exchange 2013 Standard and Enterprise CALs are available as either User or Device CALs.

For the exam, you need to be able to recommend the right level of CAL for a particular customer so it's worth learning the key functionality that is licensed by the Standard and Enterprise CALs as detailed in the next couple of paragraphs.

Exchange Standard CALs allow users to access the basic functionality of Exchange and this includes accessing their email, calendar, contacts and tasks from a variety of clients including Outlook, the Outlook Web App, or an app on a mobile device. Note that if users are accessing Exchange from a free app they do still need to license the access with a CAL. As you would expect, if users have several devices that they access the Exchange Server from, then User CALs are a good recommendation.

An Enterprise CAL adds on access to some more sophisticated features, and the most well-known is perhaps Unified Messaging which allows users to receive both emails and voice-mails into their Inboxes.

In addition, the Enterprise CAL is available "with Services". You should assume for the purposes of the exam that the Enterprise CAL includes these services which licenses users for the following:

- Data Loss Prevention (DLP) – this enforces compliance requirements for sensitive data so that important data can't be emailed or it's checked against a template before emailing, for example

- Exchange Online Protection – providing anti-malware and anti-spam services

Exchange Server 2013 Server Editions

Exchange Server 2013 is available in Standard and Enterprise editions. The Standard edition is the base level edition with the Enterprise edition offering a greater level of scalability. Technically, this is achieved by the number of mailbox databases that are supported with Standard edition supporting up to 5, and Enterprise up to 100 per server.

Note that the edition of the server license is a completely separate purchasing decision for the customer from the CALs. They do NOT need Enterprise CALs with an Enterprise Server license for example! When you're making a recommendation in the exam, consider the scalability needs first and decide on the server edition, then consider the functionality required by the users and decide on the CALs required.

Licensing Virtualized Environments

As with Project Server 2013, an Exchange Server 2013 license is assigned to a physical server and a single Exchange Server 2013 license can be used to license Exchange running in either a physical or a virtual machine.

Licensing External Users

There was a licensing change for Exchange Server with the release of the 2013 version of the product. Previously, External Connector licenses were required to license external users, but now the Server license itself covers an unlimited number of external users for access to the basic functionality of the server. If external users require access to the advanced functionality of the server then they must be licensed with Standard and Enterprise CALs.

Applying your knowledge in the exam:

- Be ready to recommend Server and CAL editions confidently. You may be asked to recommend licenses for a large company utilizing a fundamental set of technology, for which you'd need to choose the Enterprise Server (for the scalability) and Standard CALs (for the functionality)

- Remember, there is no situation where the Additive CALs can be purchased without a Base CAL. However tempting a particular answer looks, always make sure that your recommendation includes the Standard CALs

- Look out for a business need for Unified Messaging since this drives a requirement for Exchange Standard and Enterprise CALs,

- Also look out for business goals that relate to Data Loss Prevention or a specific need for anti-malware as this will also lead you to recommend the Enterprise CAL

- Make sure that you're confident with the rules for licensing Exchange 2013 in a virtualized environment so that you calculate the licenses required for a given scenario

- If you were familiar with Exchange 2010 licensing remember that there is no External Connector for Exchange 2013, the Server license covers external users for basic access. If the external users need access to advanced functionality, then recommend Standard and Enterprise CALs and in either case don't forget to include a Windows Server External Connector in your recommendations

- Don't be misled by information about the existing infrastructure of a customer that states that users are using a free app to access the services of the Exchange Server – they will still need CALs

- Look out for information that would steer you to recommend either User or Device CALs and don't forget that it's OK to mix them across an organization

SharePoint Server 2013

SharePoint Server 2013 is a content management, workflow automation, and collaboration portal, which also allows a single infrastructure for Internet, intranet and extranet sites. Users typically connect to the SharePoint sites or portals through a web browser.

Licensing SharePoint Server 2013

SharePoint Server 2013 is licensed with the Server / CAL model and, as with Exchange Server 2013, there are Standard and Enterprise CALs available to license access to different functionality.

SharePoint Standard CALs allow access to a base level of functionality across the SharePoint workloads. Key features that are enabled when users have Enterprise CALs are the full set of Search functionality and the Business Intelligence (BI) functionality, and these are key words to look for when you're deciding what CALs to recommend.

Licensing Virtualized Environments

In common with Project Server and Exchange Server, a SharePoint Server license is assigned to a physical server and then allows SharePoint to run on that machine, either in the physical environment or in a single virtual machine.

Licensing External Users

As with Exchange Server 2013, the licensing of external users changed with the release of SharePoint 2013. It's similar to the rules for Exchange Server 2013, but the Server license covers any number of external users for any level of access. However, there's another nuance with SharePoint Server licensing that you need to know about – how intranet, extranet, and Internet scenarios are licensed.

In an **intranet** scenario, a Server license is assigned to the server and all internal users (or devices) are licensed with CALs. There are no licensing requirements for the external users since they do not have access to the SharePoint content.

In an **extranet** scenario, a Server license is again assigned to the server and all internal users (or devices) are licensed with CALs. This time external users do have access, but there are again no licensing requirements because access to the server is covered by the Server license.

In an **internet** scenario, a Server license is, as usual, assigned to the server, and in this scenario there are no additional licensing requirements for either the internal or the external users. This relaxing of the licensing requirements is allowed since external users have access to all of the content on the SharePoint server.

Required Infrastructure Products

SQL Server is a required infrastructure product for SharePoint Server, and so any licensing recommendations you make for SharePoint Server should also include licenses for SQL Server which can be covered with either Core licenses or Server and CALs.

Applying your knowledge in the exam:

- Remember, as with Exchange Server 2013, that customers can never have Enterprise CALs without Standard CALs, and may mix Device and User CALs as required

- Look out for business goals for a content management, workflow automation, or collaboration solution which will lead you to recommend SharePoint as a product

- Learn the licenses required for Internet, intranet and extranet scenarios so that you can confidently recommend the right solution

- Business goals for advanced Search capabilities or a Business Intelligence solution will lead you to recommend the Enterprise CALs

- If you're asked to make a licensing recommendation for the whole technology stack make sure you include SQL Server

Lync Server 2013

Lync Server 2013 is the server solution for instant messaging, presence information, web conferencing, and enterprise telephony. There are a variety of clients that users can use to access the services of Lync Server 2013, but for the purposes of the exam you should assume that they are using the full Lync 2013 client, most commonly acquired as part of Office Professional Plus 2013.

Licensing Lync Server 2013

Lync Server 2013 actually has three CALs available for customers to purchase. There's the Base CAL which is the Standard CAL, and then two Additive CALs called the Enterprise and Plus CALs. All Lync Server users need to be licensed with the Standard CAL and then the organization can choose to purchase them Enterprise and/or Plus CALs dependent on what functionality those users need to use.

The diagram below shows users licensed with a variety of CALs dependent on what they will be doing with Lync Server, with the Standard CAL and corresponding server functionality shown in the darkest color, the Plus CAL and functionality shown in the lightest color, and the Enterprise CAL and functionality in the color in between.

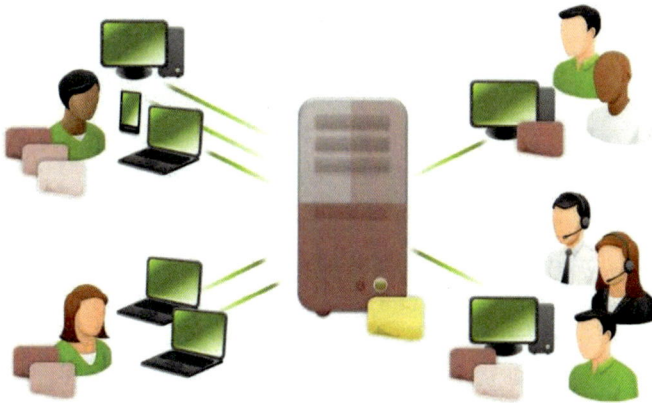

Figure 18: Lync Server 2013 Licensing

Organizations purchase Lync Standard CALs when they want to license their users for the instant messaging and integrated presence functionality of Lync Server. If they want their users to be able to set up web conferences they optionally purchase the Lync Enterprise CAL. And finally, the Plus CAL licenses users for the enterprise telephony functionality.

Licensing Virtualized Environments
Again, a single Lync Server 2013 license is assigned to a physical server and Lync is then licensed to run in either the physical environment or a virtual machine.

External Users
The Lync Server 2013 license is assigned to a physical server and an unlimited number of external users can access the services of the server.

Required Infrastructure Products
SQL Server is a required infrastructure product for Lync Server 2013, and so any licensing recommendations you make for Lync Server should also include licenses for SQL Server which can be covered with either Core licenses or Server and CALs.

Applying your knowledge in the exam:

- Remember that there are three CALs, but the Enterprise and Plus CALs are both additive to the Standard CAL. If a customer wants enterprise telephony to reduce the cost of long distance calls you can recommend the Standard CAL and the Plus CAL – they don't need the Enterprise CAL as well

- Make sure that you're familiar with the product descriptions for all of the productivity servers (Project, Exchange, SharePoint, Lync) so that you can pick out the right product against a set of business goals and requirements. Be particularly careful with business goals that state that there is a need to collaborate – is it on a document (choose SharePoint) or is it real-time person-to-person collaboration (choose Lync)?

- Learn the points outlined above regarding what the different CALs give access to; you may be asked, for example, what an organization would need to purchase if they wanted all their users to have access to setting up web conferences. You need to feel confident that this is Lync as a product, and that this particular functionality is licensed with the Standard and Enterprise CALs

- Finally, remember to include SQL Server in your licensing recommendations if you are asked to details licenses for the whole technology stack

The CAL Suites

Many customers buy one of two suites of CALs for convenience and cost-effectiveness. These suites are the Core CAL Suite and the Enterprise CAL Suite and it's worth being confident with the components of these suites for the exam. The components of the Core and Enterprise CAL Suites do change and what is listed below are the components that were part of the CAL Suites when the exam was created. CAL Suites can be purchased for Users or Devices.

	Core Infrastructure	Productivity Servers
Core CAL Suite	• Windows Server 2012 CAL • System Center 2012 R2 Configuration Manager Client Management License (CML) • System Center 2012 R2 Endpoint Protection Subscription License (SL)	• Exchange Server 2013 Standard CAL • SharePoint Server 2013 Standard CAL • Lync Server 2013 Standard CAL
Enterprise CAL Suite	• Windows Server 2012 Active Directory Rights Management Services CAL • System Center 2012 R2 Client Management Suite CML	• Exchange Server 2013 Enterprise CAL with Services • SharePoint Server 2013 Enterprise CAL • Lync Server 2013 Enterprise CAL • Exchange Online Archiving for Exchange Server SL

Figure 19: The Core and Enterprise CAL Suites

The only component in the table above that we haven't covered so far is Exchange Online Archiving for Exchange Server. This is (as its name indeed suggests!) an online archive for an on-premises deployment of Exchange Server and offers two key benefits:

- In-place archive – allowing users to store messages in an archive mailbox rather than a personal store (pst) file

- In-place hold – this preserves all mailbox content, including deleted items and original versions of modified items. This feature is important in the event of litigation

Applying your knowledge in the exam:

- As well as knowing the components that ARE in the suites, it's worth noting a couple that are omitted. In particular, be aware that a SQL CAL, a Remote Desktop Services (RDS) CAL and the Lync Plus CAL would all be additional purchases outside of the suites for organizations that need the functionality licensed by these CALs

- If one of the fictional organizations needs to make use of the basic functionality in the productivity servers (Exchange, SharePoint and Lync) then they will need the Standard CALs which are all in the Core CAL Suite. As soon as advanced functionality is mentioned you will need to recommend Enterprise CALs and thus the Enterprise CAL Suite

- A point worth noting is that these CAL Suites cannot be purchased without SA, so unless you're specifically told that an organization's agreement has expired, you can assume that a customer with one of these Suites is licensed to access the latest servers

- Look carefully at the organization's requirements for CALs; typically you should be recommending the Core CAL Suite, rather than purchasing individual CALs, if the customer has a requirement for three or more of the components

SQL Server 2014

SQL Server, as a quick definition, is Microsoft's enterprise database solution which shouldn't be confused with Microsoft Access which is a database solution for end users. There are several editions of SQL Server 2014 available to purchase, but only three that you need to know about for the exam: Standard, Business Intelligence, and Enterprise editions. You need to be clear on how each edition is licensed and, given a sample server, what licenses you should assign to it, which may vary depending on a customer's specific needs.

Server / CAL Licensing

SQL Server 2014 Business Intelligence edition is licensed with the Server / CAL model and a customer may choose to license Standard edition with either this model or the Core licensing model, detailed below.

There is only one CAL available for SQL Server 2014 which is available as either a User or a Device CAL which makes the licensing very simple: assign a Standard or BI Server license to a physical server and then assign CALs to either users or devices which need to access the services of the server.

Core Licensing

SQL Server 2014 Enterprise edition is licensed with the Core licensing model and a customer may choose to license Standard edition with either this model or the Server / CAL model, detailed above.

The Core licensing model requires you to assign licenses to a physical server based on the number of cores in the server. There's a simple rule for working out the number of Core licenses required: you count the total number of cores in the physical server, multiply this by the "Core Factor" and then assign that number of licenses to the server.

You can find the different Core Factors in the Core Factor Table document – just search for "Microsoft Core Factor Table" in your favorite Search engine – and you'll find the Core Factor Table as shown below:

Processor Type	Core Factor
All processors not mentioned below	1
AMD 31XX, 32XX, 33XX, 41XX, 42XX, 43XX, 61XX, 62XX, 63XX Series Processors with 6 or more cores	0.75
Dual Core Processors	2
Single Core Processors	4

Figure 20: Core Factor Table

So, let's take an example of an Intel server with two processors, each with four cores. Counting the total number of cores gives 2 x 4 = 8 cores. Then looking at the Core Factor table we see that the Core Factor for this type of machine would be 1, and thus 8 x 1 gives us a total of 8 licenses that are required for the server. You can see these 8 Core licenses assigned to the server below, and when they are used there is no further requirement to license access by either internal or external users or devices:

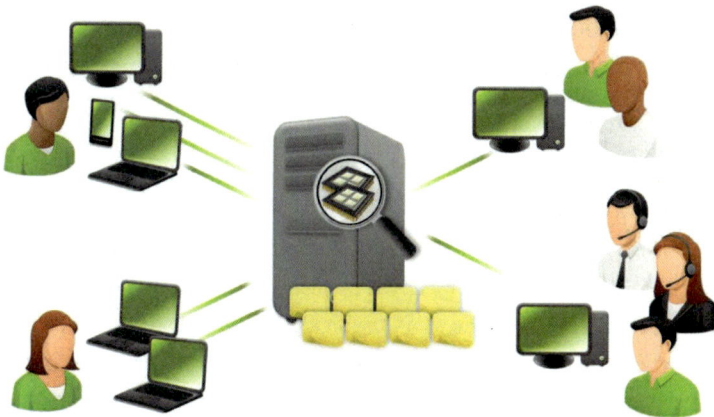

Figure 21: Core Licensing

If the processor was not an Intel processor but an AMD one that is listed in the Core Factor Table above, then the Core Factor is 0.75. If we take a server with a single processor with six cores and multiply it by the Core Factor then the answer is 4.5 – but should you assign 4 licenses to the server or 5? As you may well have guessed, the answer is 5.

There are two other points to make about Core licenses. The first is that there is always a minimum of 4 Core licenses that must be assigned to a server, regardless of how many cores it has, and the second is that Core licenses are sold in packs of 2. So, in the first example above, 8 licenses are needed, but an order would consist of 4 of the 2-pack SKU. In the exam, make sure you are clear as to whether you are being asked how many licenses are required (8) or what would be ordered (4).

Note that in the AMD example where we needed 5 licenses, you would actually total the number of licenses across the whole estate rather than buying 2-packs and assigning them to individual machines. So if you had ten of the AMD single processor machines with six cores then you would need 50 licenses which would be 25 2-packs. If you assigned 3 2-packs on a machine by machine basis this would require you to (incorrectly) buy 30 2-packs in total.

External Users

There are no External Connector licenses available for SQL Server 2014. If a customer has chosen to license with the Server / CAL model, then they must buy CALs for external users and this does become expensive when there are many external users. It is generally more cost-effective to choose to license with the Core model if there is a large number of external users, since this will cover all internal users and any number of external users.

Licensing Virtualized Environments

There are a number of different ways of licensing SQL Server 2014 in a virtualized environment that you need to know about for the exam, so let's start with the simplest – when SQL Server 2014 is licensed with the Server / CAL model.

The editions of SQL Server 2014 that are licensed with the Server / CAL model are the Standard and Business Intelligence editions, and the licensing in a virtualized environment is exactly the same as the other products licensed with the Server / CAL model that we've talked about. As a reminder, a license is assigned to the physical server and then SQL Server can run either in the physical environment or in a single virtual machine. Other licenses can be assigned to the server to allow SQL to run in further virtual machines, if required.

Let's now turn our attention to SQL Server 2014 Standard edition when it's licensed with the Core licensing model. Strictly speaking, what I'm going to tell you here does also apply to the Enterprise edition but there are better ways of licensing Enterprise edition in a virtualized environment and so I'd recommend that you think of the following just for Standard edition.

Imagine a single processor server with four cores that has two virtual machines running SQL Server 2014 Standard. Each virtual machine has two virtual cores assigned to it. To license this scenario you need to work out the licenses required for each virtual machine and then assign the total number of licenses to the physical server. So, what are the rules? Well, you count the number of virtual cores in each virtual machine and assign that number of licenses. There are two more rules to be aware of – you don't need to use the Core Factor as you do when you license in a physical environment, and you must assign a minimum of 4 Core licenses to each virtual machine.

So, have a look at the diagram below which represents the example server we are considering. The two virtual machines are shown with their two virtual cores each, and there are 8 Core licenses assigned to the physical server: although there are only two virtual cores, a minimum of 4 Core licenses must be assigned which gives us the total of 8 Core licenses:

Figure 22: Virtualization Licensing – SQL Server 2014 Standard Core

With SQL Server 2014 Enterprise edition there is additional flexibility in licensing a virtualized environment. If you license the physical server completely then you can run SQL Server 2014 in a virtual machine for each Core license that you have assigned to the server. Consider the diagram below where you see a server with two four core processors. To license that server completely you need to assign 8 Core licenses to the physical server and then you can run SQL Server in eight virtual machines, as shown:

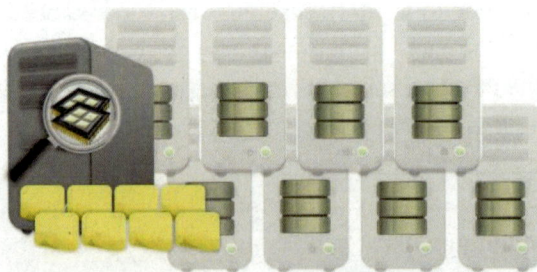

Figure 23: Virtualization Licensing – SQL Server 2014 Enterprise Core

So you can see why I'd recommend that you use the alternative method for licensing Enterprise edition: in the first example you'd have had to assign 8 licenses to be allowed to run 2 virtual machines, and in the second example you can assign 8 licenses to run eight virtual machines! Do note in the example above, you can simply add further Core licenses to the physical server to increase the number of virtual machines that you're allowed to run.

And the final part of virtualization licensing to consider is that of unlimited virtualization. This is only available for the Enterprise edition and is actually a Software Assurance benefit but I think it makes sense to include it here. The rules are simple: if you license a physical server with Enterprise Core licenses with Software Assurance then you can run an unlimited number of virtual machines with SQL Server on that server.

The server below has, again, two four core processors and so 8 Core licenses with SA need to be assigned to the server. You can see ten virtual machines running SQL Server, but an unlimited number would be allowed:

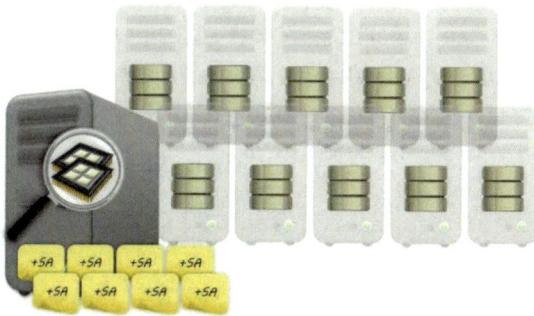

Figure 24: Unlimited Virtualization – SQL Server 2014 Enterprise Core

Applying your knowledge in the exam:

- Remember the licensing models that apply to the different editions of SQL Server 2014; you don't want to get caught out recommending a Server / CAL model for the Enterprise edition, for example

- Look out for business goals that specify that an organization wants to allow a large or unknown number of people to access their SQL Server; this is a clear steer to make a recommendation of Core licensing for SQL Server, whereas a small deployment for an organization wanting to keep costs as low as possible is likely to be a recommendation for the Server / CAL model

- Look out for business goals that state that an organization wants to give access to their SQL Server to external users – there is no additional External Connector license for SQL Server and the Core license is (certainly for the exam!) the best way to license these external users

- You need to be confident in being able to license a given server with Core licenses so make sure that you remember the exceptions: the Core Factor for AMD processors (0.75) and the minimum number of Core licenses that must be assigned (4)

- Again, you may be given a virtualized environment to specify the licenses for and this is likely to include the more complex Core licenses. So make sure that you know how Standard edition works (based on virtual cores), Enterprise edition (1 VM per Core license), and how a customer gets unlimited virtualization rights (Enterprise Core licenses with SA)

- Check very carefully whether you are being asked to recommend the total number of Core licenses in a scenario or the number of 2-packs that a customer should purchase

Dynamics CRM Server 2013

Microsoft Dynamics CRM is Microsoft's customer relationship management (CRM) solution. There are two server editions available for Dynamics CRM 2013: CRM Workgroup Server 2013 and Dynamics CRM Server 2013. This section focuses on CRM Server 2013 since the Workgroup edition, as you would expect, is aimed at smaller businesses.

Licensing Dynamics CRM Server 2013

CRM 2013 is licensed with the familiar Server / CAL model, with CALs available as either User or Device CALs for three different levels:

- Essential CAL: for light-weight access to custom applications

- Basic CAL: for basic CRM, reporting, and access to custom applications

- Professional CAL: for full sales, service and marketing use, and access to custom applications

Note that with products like Exchange Server there is a Base CAL (the Standard CAL) and then an optional Additive CAL (the Enterprise CAL) which may be purchased if required. With CRM 2013, the CALs are all separate from each other, and customers should buy the single CAL from the list above that they need.

This does beg the question as to what happens if a customer purchases an Essential CAL for a user and then finds that they actually need a Basic CAL. This is where there ARE Additive CALs for CRM 2013: you can buy a Basic Use Additive CAL which is added to an Essential CAL to give the rights of the Basic CAL, or a Professional Use Additive CAL which is added to a Basic CAL to give the rights of the Professional CAL.

Licensing Virtualized Environments

A Dynamics CRM Server 2013 license is assigned to a physical server and allows the software to be run in either the physical operating system environment or in a virtual machine running on the server.

Licensing External Users

As we saw with the productivity servers, a Server license often licenses external users and this is also the case with CRM Server 2013.

Required Infrastructure Products

SQL Server is a required infrastructure product for CRM Server 2013 so, as usual, make sure that your licensing recommendations include licenses for this product.

Applying your knowledge in the exam:

- Remember that the CRM 2013 CALs work in a different way to the Standard and Enterprise CALs for products such as SharePoint Server. With SharePoint you would need to recommend both Standard and Enterprise CALs to license access to the most advanced functionality, but with CRM you choose a single CAL that licenses the correct access

- Don't forget that there ARE some Additive CALs for CRM 2013 which allow a customer to lift the level of access for a particular user. You should recommend these Additive CALs in customer scenarios where they need to, in effect, change the CALs for their users

- As usual, learn the virtualization rules (1 VM per Server license), how external users are licensed (with the Server license), and any required infrastructure products (SQL Server)

Online Services

User Subscription Licenses (USLs) are generally available for products that have a hosted element. The licenses are always non-perpetual, just allowing access to the service as long as the subscription is active and they are always assigned to an individual user. Licenses may be reassigned between users but, in common with the on-premises software licenses, typically no more than every 90 days.

Hosted products are relatively new and are the alternative to traditional on-premises deployments of products. An on-premises deployment of Exchange would see an Exchange Server installed on a server in an organization's premises managed by the IT staff, with users using a variety of methods to access their email. A hosted deployment removes the need for the physical Exchange Server on-site since it is now hosted on Microsoft or partner servers. This is attractive to organizations since the costs of the server itself and those associated with managing it are removed. From an end user perspective the users typically access their email in the same ways as with an on-premises deployment.

Windows Intune

Windows Intune is a cloud based solution for managing PCs and mobile devices. It's an alternative to an on-premises deployment of System Center since IT staff can perform updates, deploy malware protection, and manage inventory over the web.

Licensing Windows Intune

Windows Intune is licensed with a User Subscription License and allows up to 5 devices to be managed for the licensed user. These devices can be PCs (x86 devices) or mobile devices.

Windows Intune Licenses

There are two main Windows Intune licenses that you need to know about for the exam: Windows Intune, and the Windows Intune Add-on for System Center Configuration Manager.

Windows Intune gives access to the Windows Intune cloud-based service, as well as use rights for System Center Configuration Manager and System Center Endpoint Protection.

The Windows Intune Add-on for System Center Configuration Manager is for customers who are already licensed for System Center Configuration Manager and System Center Endpoint Protection and just want to add on the Intune Service.

Applying your knowledge in the exam:

- When you're recommending which Windows Intune licenses a customer should buy take careful note of which licenses they already have since if they have one of the CAL Suites they will be eligible for the Add-on

- Remember that Windows Intune is a User Subscription License rather than a Device Subscription License so take note of the number of users when providing an Intune licensing solution

Office 365

The Office 365 Online Services consist of hosted versions of the productivity servers (Exchange, SharePoint and Lync) as well as other related services such as Yammer and OneDrive for Business, and Office 365 ProPlus. Organizations can either purchase licenses for the separate services, or groups of licenses which are known as Plans. Licenses for both the individual services and the Plans are USLs.

For the exam, you need to be familiar with the individual components as well as the key plans for businesses. Let's start by looking at the key products that make up the Office 365 family.

Office 365 ProPlus

It's tempting to think of Office 365 ProPlus as the way to acquire Office Professional Plus 2013 through a subscription program, but this is a little bit dangerous since the products differ technically and also give different use rights, although users typically won't know (or care!) which one is actually installed on their devices.

Firstly, the licensing model is different; Office Professional Plus 2013 is a device licensing model where the products are installed on a single device and the license is assigned to that device. Office 365 ProPlus is a user licensing model where the USL is assigned to a user and then that user is allowed to install the Office applications on up to 5 devices.

Another key difference is that there are no downgrade rights for Office 365 ProPlus, whereas you can install any previous version with an Office Professional Plus 2013 license.

Office 365 ProPlus includes access to Office Online (the web versions of the Office products), while for Office Professional Plus 2013 it's only available as a Software Assurance benefit.

Office 365 ProPlus users can also use Office on Demand. This service essentially temporarily installs Office on any device that the licensed user wants to use it on. The applications are removed from the device after the user has used them and this doesn't count towards their 5 installations of the product.

Finally, there are the deployment rights to consider, and these are identical: both Office Professional Plus 2013 and Office 365 ProPlus licenses allow Office to be deployed in an RDS environment, in a Virtual Desktop Infrastructure, or on a Windows To Go USB stick.

Exchange Online

Exchange Online is available as a Plan 1 or Plan 2 USL. Plan 1 corresponds broadly to the functionality you'd have access to with an Exchange Standard CAL if you were licensing an on-premises deployment, while Plan 2 is everything in Plan 1 and then access to the functionality that would correspond to the Enterprise CAL. Note that while the on-premises licensing requires you to have the Standard AND Enterprise CALs, when you buy the Exchange Online Plans, you buy EITHER Plan 1 OR Plan 2.

The Exchange Online Plans are also valid licenses to access an on-premises server as an alternative to Exchange Standard and Enterprise CALs.

SharePoint Online

SharePoint Online is available as a Plan 1 or Plan 2 USL in exactly the same way as Exchange Online above, and also gives access to an on-premises SharePoint server as an alternative to SharePoint Standard and Enterprise CALs.

Lync Online

Lync Online is very similar to Exchange Online and SharePoint Online in that there are Plan 1 and Plan 2 USLs which also allow access to Lync Server as an alternative to Lync Standard and Enterprise CALs. However, there is no Lync Online Plan which corresponds to the Plus CAL and so customers who need enterprise telephony functionality do need to have an on-premises deployment.

Yammer

Yammer is a private enterprise social network tool to help users to collaborate both internally and externally in a secure, closed network. A Yammer Enterprise USL gives access to the standalone service but most customers (in real life, and certainly for the exam) acquire Yammer as part of an Office 365 Plan.

OneDrive for Business

OneDrive for Business is a place for users to store and organize their work documents. Again, there is a OneDrive for Business USL available but most customers will acquire OneDrive for Business as part of an Office 365 Plan.

Office 365 for Developers

This is a subscription for developers who want to develop Office applications and although it is available as a separate subscription it is included in most of the Office 365 Plans and, again, that's how most customers acquire it.

The Enterprise Plans

We're familiar with the notion of Suites for collections of on-premises licenses and the equivalent in the Office 365 world are Plans which span different groups of licenses. We'll split these into two, looking first at the E Plans which are aimed at the Enterprise workers – i.e. end users in a typical organization. The diagram below shows the components that are contained in each plan and it's worth making sure that you're familiar with them so that you can easily pick out the right recommendation for a customer.

	Plan E1	Plan E3	Plan E4
Lync Plus CAL			✔
SharePoint Enterprise CAL/SharePoint Plan 2		✔	✔
Exchange Enterprise CAL/Exchange Plan 2		✔	✔
Office 365 ProPlus (inc Office on Demand)		✔	✔
Office Online	✔	✔	✔
OneDrive for Business	✔	✔	✔
Yammer Enterprise	✔	✔	✔
Lync Enterprise CAL/Lync Plan 2	✔	✔	✔
Lync Standard CAL/Lync Plan 1	✔	✔	✔
SharePoint Standard CAL/SharePoint Plan 1	✔	✔	✔
Exchange Standard CAL/Exchange Plan 1	✔	✔	✔

Figure 25: Office 365 Enterprise Plans

As we saw earlier, there is no Lync Online Plan 3 giving access to an online enterprise telephony service and so customers who purchase the E4 Plan are licensed with a Lync Plus CAL to access an on-premises deployment.

The Kiosk Plans

And finally the K Plans, where the K stands for "Kiosk" and a Kiosk worker is someone who only spends perhaps 5 to 10% of their time on a PC, and thus potentially does not need such a rich set of tools as the Enterprise worker. There is just one K Plan – K1 – and as you can see below, it consists of Exchange Online Kiosk and SharePoint Online Kiosk, which give basic access to Exchange and SharePoint Online. The Plan also includes access to Office Online for working with Office documents:

	K1
Office Online	✔
SharePoint Online Kiosk	✔
Exchange Online Kiosk	✔

Figure 26: Office 365 Kiosk Plan

Applying your knowledge in the exam:

- Look out for business goals that hint at an organization potentially finding the idea of hosted services attractive – for example, a business goal that states that the IT department don't want the hassle of managing on-premises servers, or that they want to deploy a new service but don't have any experience of setting up and managing that product

- Don't forget that Office 365 is ALWAYS licensed by user, not device, so if you're asked to recommend the number of licenses a customer needs, you need to consider the number of users, rather than the number of devices that they are using

- Look out for business goals that state an organization's preference for owning or renting licenses; if they like to own assets such as software licenses, then an Office 365 solution will not fit their needs since all the licenses are subscription licenses

- Be prepared to recommend the right Office 365 Plan for a given scenario so make sure that you're confident with the differences between them

- It's fine to mix Plans across an organization and you should look out for this in the scenarios since this would be a good, cost-effective recommendation

- Don't forget the Kiosk plan when you're thinking about recommending Plans. If an organization is trying to minimize costs it could be a hint that the K1 Plan should be recommended

- Remember that the standalone Plans for Exchange, SharePoint, and Lync Online work in exactly the opposite way to the equivalent on-premises CALs in that a customer should buy Exchange Online Plan 1 OR Plan 2 – never both. Make sure that you never recommend Plan 1 AND Plan 2 for a customer to have access to the highest level of functionality

- Look out for business goals that state that an organization wants to be able to access SharePoint sites that have been deployed on on-premises servers as well as ones deployed via SharePoint Online. The SharePoint Online USLs include dual access rights so you should never recommend that a customer needs SharePoint CALs AND SharePoint Online Plans. Note that this applies to Exchange and Lync too

- Make sure that you learn the different use rights that Office Professional Plus 2013 and Office 365 ProPlus give. In particular, remember that Office 365 ProPlus does not give downgrade rights and watch out for a requirement for this in the business goals section of the customer scenario

- If you're asked to choose between recommending Office 365 ProPlus and Office Professional Plus 2013, remember that where there are more devices than users, Office 365 ProPlus is likely to be the most cost-effective recommendation

Enterprise Mobility Suite

The Enterprise Mobility Suite was launched by Microsoft in April 2014 to deliver on their mobile first, cloud first vision. If you're not familiar with this, it's essentially the notion that these days we all want to use multiple devices in lots of different locations and to have access to pretty much the same stuff across all of those devices with a high level of synchronization. Microsoft believe that the chief way of managing this mobile experience is through the cloud, and this is where the Enterprise Mobility Suite, or EMS, comes in.

The EMS Technologies

This diagram shows the technical requirements to deliver on this vision in the left hand column and the actual Microsoft technology that needs to be used in the right hand column. It's these technologies that form the Enterprise Mobility Suite:

Requirement	Technology
Identity and Access Management	Azure Active Directory Premium
Mobile Device Management	Windows Intune
Mobile Application Management	
Information Protection	Azure Rights Management Services

Figure 27: The Enterprise Mobility Suite

Licensing EMS

The Enterprise Mobility Suite is available as an Add-on USL for customers who have active Software Assurance on the Core or Enterprise CAL Suite, or any of the CAL Suite Bridges for Office 365.

These licenses are called qualifying licenses and it's absolutely fine for a customer to have a device Core CAL Suite and then to add on the EMS USL. What's not permissible though is to have more Add-ons than the underlying licenses – if a customer has 500 Core CAL Suite licenses then they would be able to buy a maximum of 500 EMS Add-ons, for example.

Applying your knowledge in the exam:

- Remember that the EMS license is an Add-on license and so if you recommend it in a particular customer scenario check that there are underlying qualifying licenses available. On the same note, check that the Software Assurance is active too

- Learn the different components of the Enterprise Mobility Suite so that you don't over-recommend licenses. For example, a customer would not need to purchase a USL for both Windows Intune and the EMS Add-on

Microsoft Azure Services

The Microsoft Azure Services are an ever-growing collection of Microsoft-hosted cloud services. Examples of these services would be having virtual machines hosted on Microsoft's servers, or a website hosted there, or even just using it as an off-site data storage facility. You don't need to be an expert on the different services for the exam, you just need to know how customers license these services.

User Subscription Licenses

Azure Services are licensed in two main ways. The first is via a User Subscription License, and an example of this is Azure Rights Management Services which is part of the Enterprise Mobility Suite as we saw in the previous section. A monthly fee is paid which activates the service for a particular user.

Consumption Based Services

The second way to buy and license Azure is on a consumption basis and I think it's best to take a practical example at this point. One service available through Azure is to purchase a Windows Server virtual machine – you simply decide on the resources you want the virtual machine to have in terms of the number of cores and the amount of RAM etc. in much the same way you would if you went to a hardware supplier and ordered a physical machine. As you would expect, the higher specification the Azure virtual machine has, the more it costs. An Azure Windows Server virtual machine includes the cost of the Windows Server license and there are no requirements for CALs. It's offered on an hourly rate, which allows you to only pay for the server while it's up and running.

You can imagine this makes it a very attractive proposition for a development and test environment since servers can be set up for a short term project and then turned off when they're no longer needed. The alternative would have been to have purchased new hardware which is unused when the project ends, and to purchase licenses which, again, could potentially end up being unused for periods of time.

The Azure Services available to be purchased through the consumption model can be bought directly from Microsoft through the customer portal, but for the purposes of the exam you should focus on how they are purchased by customers through the Volume Licensing agreements – either as an Additional Product in the Enterprise Agreement or through the Server and Cloud Enrollment, and there's more detail on these programs in the next section.

Applying your knowledge in the exam:

- Look out for details in a customer scenario that state that an IT team want some short-term test or development servers since this would lead to a recommendation to deploy the servers on Azure rather than buying new hardware and licenses

CRM Online

CRM Online is the online version of Dynamics CRM Server 2013 offering the same customer relationship management functionality.

Licensing CRM Online

In common with the CALs for CRM Server 2013, there are different levels of access to the core CRM functionality that may be licensed and in the case of CRM Online this is, of course, done with USLs. The following USLs are available:

- Essential USL: for light-weight access to custom applications

- Basic USL: for basic CRM, reporting, and access to custom applications

- Professional USL: for full sales, service and marketing use, and access to custom applications

- Enterprise USL: includes access to Microsoft Dynamics Marketing and Microsoft Social Listening capabilities

In a parallel licensing model with the on-premises licensing there are also Step Up USLs available for users licensed, for example, with the Essential USL who subsequently need access to the features licensed by the Basic USL.

Applying your knowledge in the exam:

- The CRM Online USLs are not included in any of the Office 365 Plans so make sure that you include these USLs as additional licensing recommendations

- Remember that there are full USLs and then Step Up USLs to move from one USL to another so there is flexibility if a customer's requirements change

The Microsoft Products and their Licensing Models Revision Cards

Let me introduce you to our Revision Cards. We thought it would be useful to have a recap or summary section which covers all the key points that you need to know for the exam so we decided on a series of "cards" – or tables that you can work through just to remind yourself of the key points that you need to know from this section. You'll see that the following cards have all the products that we've looked at with key notes on how they're licensed.

Revision Card 1:
Licensing Windows 8.1

Product	Description	Licensing Model
Windows 8.1 Pro	Microsoft client operating system entry level edition for businesses	Per Device
Windows 8.1 Enterprise	Microsoft client operating system with further features (AppLocker, BranchCache, DirectAccess) for businesses	Per Device

Revision Card 2:
Rights of Windows 8.1 Licenses

	OEM	Volume Licensing	
Editions available	Windows 8.1 Pro	Windows 8.1 Pro Upgrade	Windows 8.1 Enterprise Upgrade
Can add Software Assurance	No	No	Yes
License reassignment rights	None	None	Yes, if the license has active SA
Downgrade rights	Windows 7 Professional Windows Vista Business	Any previous Professional version	Any previous version of any edition

Revision Card 3:
Office 2013 Products

Product	Description	Licensing Model
Word 2013	A word-processing tool	Per Device
Excel 2013	A spreadsheet tool	Per Device
PowerPoint 2013	A graphics and presentation tool	Per Device
Outlook 2013	The email client with calendar, tasks and contacts functionality	Per Device
OneNote 2013	A note-taking and information gathering application	Per Device
Publisher 2013	A desktop publishing tool	Per Device
Access 2013	The end user database solution	Per Device
Lync 2013	The client application for the Lync Server product	Per Device
InfoPath 2013	An application for building and consuming electronic forms	Per Device
Visio 2013	An Office family product for creating sophisticated diagrams	Per Device
Project 2013	An Office family product for creating project plans	Per Device

Revision Card 4:
Editions of Office 2013

	Office Standard 2013	Office Professional 2013	Office Professional Plus 2013
Word 2013	✓	✓	✓
Excel 2013	✓	✓	✓
PowerPoint 2013	✓	✓	✓
Outlook 2013	✓	✓	✓
OneNote 2013	✓	✓	✓
Publisher 2013	✓	✓	✓
Access 2013		✓	✓
Lync 2013			✓
InfoPath 2013			✓

Revision Card 5:
Rights of Office 2013 Licenses

	OEM	Volume Licensing	
Editions available	Office Professional 2013	Office Standard 2013	Office Professional Plus 2013
Can add Software Assurance	Yes (Standard) within 90 days	Yes at point of purchase	Yes at point of purchase
License reassignment rights	None	Yes	Yes
Downgrade rights	None	Any previous version of Standard	Any previous version of Professional Plus
Portable Use Rights	No	Yes	Yes
Network Usage Rights	No	Yes	Yes
Enhanced Server Integration	No	Part	Full

Revision Card 6:

Licensing a Virtual Desktop Infrastructure

Situation	Windows and Office Licenses Required License all users with Windows and RDS User CALs	
Corporate-owned x86 device used anywhere		Windows SA and Office SA
Third party-owned device used off-premises by primary user		Covered by Roaming Use Rights of licenses above for primary user
Corporate-owned non-x86 device used anywhere		Windows VDA and Office
Corporate-owned non-x86 companion device used anywhere		Windows SA, CSL and Office on primary device Office on companion device
Third party-owned devices used on-premises		Windows SA and CSL on primary device Office 365 ProPlus USL for primary user

Revision Card 7:
Licensing Windows Server 2012 R2

Product	Licensing Model	Virtualization Rights
Windows Server 2012 R2 Standard	One Processor-based license covers up to two processors in a physical server. All processors must be licensed	2 virtual machines for every Processor-based license
Windows Server 2012 R2 Datacenter	External users can be licensed with CALs or with a single External Connector license per server	Unlimited virtual machines

Revision Card 8:
Licensing Windows Server 2012 R2 Services

Product	Description	Licensing Model
Windows Server 2012 Remote Desktop Services	Service of Windows Server to allow an organization to install and run applications on a server	RDS CAL RDS External Connector for external users
Windows Server 2012 Active Directory Rights Management Services	Service of Windows Server giving Information Rights Management capabilities to prevent documents being copied or printed, for example	AD RMS CAL AD RMS External Connector for external users

Revision Card 9:
System Center 2012 R2 Server Management Licenses

Product	Licensing Model	Virtualization Rights
System Center 2012 R2 Standard	One Processor-based license covers up to two processors in a physical server. All processors must be licensed	2 virtual machines may be managed for every Processor-based license
System Center 2012 R2 Datacenter	External users can be licensed with CALs or with an External Connector license	Unlimited virtual machines may be managed

Revision Card 10:
System Center 2012 R2 Client Management Licenses

Client Management License	CAL Suite
System Center 2012 R2 Configuration Manager CML	Core CAL Suite
System Center 2012 R2 Endpoint Protection SL	Core CAL Suite
System Center 2012 R2 Client Management Suite CML	Enterprise CAL Suite

Revision Card 11:
Licensing the Productivity Servers

Product	Description	Licensing Model
Exchange Server 2013	The email server	Server / CAL • Standard CALs • Enterprise CALs (Unified Messaging, DLP, anti-malware) External users: Server license, or Standard + Enterprise CALs for advanced access
SharePoint Server 2013	A content management, workflow, and collaboration portal, which also allows a single infrastructure for Internet, intranet and extranet sites	Server / CAL • Standard CALs • Enterprise CALs (Advanced Search, BI) External users: Server license SQL Server required
Lync Server 2013	The server solution for instant messaging, presence information, web conferencing, and enterprise telephony	Server / CAL • Standard CALs (IM, presence) • Enterprise CALs (web conferencing) • Plus CALs (enterprise telephony) External users: Server license SQL Server required
Project Server 2013	A project management server solution	Server / CAL External users: CALs SQL Server and SharePoint Server required

Revision Card 12:
The CAL Suites

	Core Infrastructure	Productivity Servers
Core CAL Suite	• Windows Server 2012 CAL • System Center 2012 R2 Configuration Manager Client Management License (CML) • System Center 2012 R2 Endpoint Protection Subscription License (SL)	• Exchange Server 2013 Standard CAL • SharePoint Server 2013 Standard CAL • Lync Server 2013 Standard CAL
Enterprise CAL Suite	• Windows Server 2012 Active Directory Rights Management Services CAL • System Center 2012 R2 Client Management Suite CML	• Exchange Server 2013 Enterprise CAL with Services • SharePoint Server 2013 Enterprise CAL • Lync Server 2013 Enterprise CAL • Exchange Online Archiving for Exchange Server SL

Revision Card 13:
Licensing SQL Server 2014

Edition	Licensing Model	Virtualization Licensing
Standard	Server / CAL	1 VM per Server license
Standard	Per Core • Calculate total cores in the server and multiply by the Core Factor	Per VM based on virtual cores with a minimum of 4 licenses
Business Intelligence	Server / CAL	1 VM per Server license
Enterprise	Per Core • Calculate total cores in the server and multiply by the Core Factor	License physical server • 1 VM per Core license • Add SA for unlimited virtualization

Revision Card 14:
Licensing Dynamics CRM Server 2013

Licensing Model	CALs Available
Server / CAL External users: Server license SQL Server required	Standalone CALs • Essential CAL • Basic CAL • Professional CAL Additive CALs • Basic Use Additive CAL • Professional Use Additive CAL

Revision Card 15:
Licensing Windows Intune

Description	Licenses Available
A cloud based solution for managing up to 5 PCs and mobile devices per licensed user	• Windows Intune USL • Windows Intune Add-on for System Center Configuration Manager USL

Revision Card 16:
Office 365 Enterprise Plans

	Plan E1	Plan E3	Plan E4
Lync Plus CAL			✔
SharePoint Enterprise CAL/SharePoint Plan 2		✔	✔
Exchange Enterprise CAL/Exchange Plan 2		✔	✔
Office 365 ProPlus (inc Office on Demand)		✔	✔
Office Online	✔	✔	✔
OneDrive for Business	✔	✔	✔
Yammer Enterprise	✔	✔	✔
Lync Enterprise CAL/Lync Plan 2	✔	✔	✔
Lync Standard CAL/Lync Plan 1	✔	✔	✔
SharePoint Standard CAL/SharePoint Plan 1	✔	✔	✔
Exchange Standard CAL/Exchange Plan 1	✔	✔	✔

Revision Card 17:
Office 365 Kiosk Plan

	K1
Office Online	✔
SharePoint Online Kiosk	✔
Exchange Online Kiosk	✔

Revision Card 18:
Enterprise Mobility Suite Add-on USL

Qualifying Licenses	Requirement	Technology
Core CAL Suite Enterprise CAL Suite	Identity and Access Management	Azure Active Directory Premium
Any Core CAL or Enterprise CAL Suite Bridge for Office 365	Mobile Device Management	Windows Intune
	Mobile Application Management	
	Information Protection	Azure Rights Management Services

Revision Card 19:
Licensing CRM Online

Full USLs	Step Up USLs
Essential USL	Essential to Basic, Professional or Enterprise
Basic USL	Basic to Professional or Enterprise
Professional USL	Professional to Enterprise
Enterprise USL	

Recap Questions and Answers

Use these Recap Questions to see how much you know about the Microsoft products and their licensing. If you find any areas that you need to go over you can review the relevant topic in this section of the book. You'll find a couple of questions on each page with the answers when you turn over.

Questions 1 – 4

1. The IT manager at Periwinkle Packaging Solutions is looking into a document management system. What product is likely to fit his needs?
   a) SharePoint Server 2013
   b) Project Server 2013
   c) Exchange Server 2013
   d) Lync Server 2013

2. Taupe Telecoms have set up an online ordering system and want to allow an unlimited number of users to access their SQL Server 2014 deployment. How would you recommend that they license this product?
   a) With Processor licenses
   b) With Core licenses
   c) With an External Connector license
   d) With a Web Extension license

3. Blue Lamp Ideas are about to deploy Exchange Server 2013 where they want their employees to be able to make use of the full set of features that Exchange offers. What licenses will they need to purchase? Choose three answers.
   a) Exchange Server license
   b) Exchange CALs for all users
   c) Exchange Standard CALs for all users
   d) Exchange Enterprise CALs for all users
   e) Exchange External Connector license

4. Which of the following rights does an Office 365 ProPlus USL give? Choose three answers.
   a) Rights to use Office Online
   b) Rights to use Office on Demand
   c) Downgrade rights
   d) Rights to deploy Office in a VDI environment
   e) Rights to deploy Office on an unlimited number of machines

Answers 1 – 4

1. The IT manager at Periwinkle Packaging Solutions is looking into a document management system. What product is likely to fit his needs?
   a) **SharePoint Server 2013** ✓
   b) Project Server 2013
   c) Exchange Server 2013
   d) Lync Server 2013

2. Taupe Telecoms have set up an online ordering system and want to allow an unlimited number of users to access their SQL Server 2014 deployment. How would you recommend that they license this product?
   a) With Processor licenses
   b) **With Core licenses** ✓
   c) With an External Connector license
   d) With a Web Extension license

3. Blue Lamp Ideas are about to deploy Exchange Server 2013 where they want their employees to be able to make use of the full set of features that Exchange offers. What licenses will they need to purchase? Choose three answers.
   a) **Exchange Server license** ✓
   b) Exchange CALs for all users
   c) **Exchange Standard CALs for all users** ✓
   d) **Exchange Enterprise CALs for all users** ✓
   e) Exchange External Connector license

4. Which of the following rights does an Office 365 ProPlus USL give? Choose three answers.
   a) **Rights to use Office Online** ✓
   b) **Rights to use Office on Demand** ✓
   c) Downgrade rights
   d) **Rights to deploy Office in a VDI environment** ✓
   e) Rights to deploy Office on an unlimited number of machines

Questions 5 – 7

5. The IT Manager at The Papaya Hire Company wants to purchase Office 365 for all of his users. He has 350 users and 335 devices. How should he license Office 365?

a) With Office 365 DSLs
b) With Office 365 USLs
c) With Office 365 Device CALs
d) With Office 365 User CALs

6. Almond Retail have 1,050 PCs which are used by 1,265 users. All users make use of Windows 8.1 and Office 2013 on the PCs. What licenses should Almond Retail purchase?

a) 1,050 Windows 8.1 licenses and 1,050 Office 2013 licenses
b) 1,050 Windows 8.1 licenses and 1,265 Office 2013 licenses
c) 1,265 Windows 8.1 licenses and 1,050 Office 2013 licenses
d) 1,265 Windows 8.1 licenses and 1,265 Office 2013 licenses

7. Fuchsia Fancy Dress Hire have a four-processor server running Windows Server 2012 R2 Standard in six virtual machines. How many Windows Server 2012 R2 Standard licenses should they assign to the server?

a) 2
b) 3
c) 4
d) 6

Answers 5 – 7

5. The IT Manager at The Papaya Hire Company wants to purchase Office 365 for all of his users. He has 350 users and 335 devices. How should he license Office 365?

    a) With Office 365 DSLs
    b) With Office 365 USLs ✓
    c) With Office 365 Device CALs
    d) With Office 365 User CALs

6. Almond Retail have 1,050 PCs which are used by 1,265 users. All users make use of Windows 8.1 and Office 2013 on the PCs. What licenses should Almond Retail purchase?

    a) 1,050 Windows 8.1 licenses and 1,050 Office 2013 licenses ✓
    b) 1,050 Windows 8.1 licenses and 1,265 Office 2013 licenses
    c) 1,265 Windows 8.1 licenses and 1,050 Office 2013 licenses
    d) 1,265 Windows 8.1 licenses and 1,265 Office 2013 licenses

7. Fuchsia Fancy Dress Hire have a four-processor server running Windows Server 2012 R2 Standard in six virtual machines. How many Windows Server 2012 R2 Standard licenses should they assign to the server?

    a) 2
    b) 3 ✓
    c) 4
    d) 6

Questions 8 – 10

8. Lilac Landscaping Services are intending to deploy their website using SharePoint Server 2013 on a dedicated server. What licenses do they need for this server so that external users are licensed to access the site and the content on it? Choose three answers.

   a) SharePoint Server 2013 External Connector license
   b) SharePoint Server 2013 for Internet Sites license
   c) SharePoint Server 2013 license
   d) Windows Server 2012 R2 license
   e) Windows Server 2012 External Connector license

9. Ultramarine Swim Wear have some servers that are running a large number of virtual machines that all need to be managed using System Center 2012 R2. What should they license the servers with?

   a) System Center 2012 R2 Client Management Suite
   b) System Center 2012 R2 Server Management Suite
   c) System Center 2012 R2 Standard Server Management Licenses
   d) System Center 2012 R2 Datacenter Server Management Licenses

10. Pink Champagne Limousines have deployed Exchange Server 2013 throughout their organization and have a significant number of external users who need to access the server too for basic email. How should Pink Champagne Limousines license their external users?

   a) With an Exchange Server license
   b) With an Exchange External Connector license
   c) With User CALs
   d) With Device CALs

8. Lilac Landscaping Services are intending to deploy their website using SharePoint Server 2013 on a dedicated server. What licenses do they need for this server so that external users are licensed to access the site and the content on it? Choose three answers.

   a) SharePoint Server 2013 External Connector license
   b) SharePoint Server 2013 for Internet Sites license
   c) **SharePoint Server 2013 license** ✓
   d) **Windows Server 2012 R2 license** ✓
   e) **Windows Server 2012 External Connector license** ✓

9. Ultramarine Swim Wear have some servers that are running a large number of virtual machines that all need to be managed using System Center 2012 R2. What should they license the servers with?

   a) System Center 2012 R2 Client Management Suite
   b) System Center 2012 R2 Server Management Suite
   c) System Center 2012 R2 Standard Server Management Licenses
   d) **System Center 2012 R2 Datacenter Server Management Licenses** ✓

10. Pink Champagne Limousines have deployed Exchange Server 2013 throughout their organization and have a significant number of external users who need to access the server too for basic email. How should Pink Champagne Limousines license their external users?

    a) **With an Exchange Server license** ✓
    b) With an Exchange External Connector license
    c) With User CALs
    d) With Device CALs

Questions 11 – 13

11. The IT Manager at Cyan Ida's Pharmacy likes the idea of having hosted management and security services for his devices and has decided to purchase Windows Intune licenses. He has 515 devices in the organization that are used by 625 users. What licenses should he purchase?

a) 625 Windows Intune USLs
b) 515 Windows Intune DSLs
c) 515 Windows Intune Security and Management SLs
d) 625 Windows Intune User CALs

12. Apple and Pears Stairlifts have deployed a sophisticated workflow solution based on SharePoint Server 2013 throughout their organization and now need to buy the relevant CALs for their users. What CALs should they purchase?

a) SharePoint Enterprise CALs
b) SharePoint Standard and Enterprise CALs
c) SharePoint CALs
d) SharePoint Datacenter CALs

13. The Cobalt Bolt Company have a large data warehouse application based on SQL Server 2014 which will be accessed by many hundreds of external users. What edition of SQL Server 2014 is likely to be the best purchase for them?

a) Standard
b) Enterprise
c) Datacenter
d) Warehouse

11. The IT Manager at Cyan Ida's Pharmacy likes the idea of having hosted management and security services for his devices and has decided to purchase Windows Intune licenses. He has 515 devices in the organization that are used by 625 users. What licenses should he purchase?

    a) **625 Windows Intune USLs** ✓
    b) 515 Windows Intune DSLs
    c) 515 Windows Intune Security and Management SLs
    d) 625 Windows Intune User CALs

12. Apple and Pears Stairlifts have deployed a sophisticated workflow solution based on SharePoint Server 2013 throughout their organization and now need to buy the relevant CALs for their users. What CALs should they purchase?

    a) SharePoint Enterprise CALs
    b) **SharePoint Standard and Enterprise CALs** ✓
    c) SharePoint CALs
    d) SharePoint Datacenter CALs

13. The Cobalt Bolt Company have a large data warehouse application based on SQL Server 2014 which will be accessed by many hundreds of external users. What edition of SQL Server 2014 is likely to be the best purchase for them?

    a) Standard
    b) **Enterprise** ✓
    c) Datacenter
    d) Warehouse

Questions 14 – 16

14. World of Magnolia have 850 PCs that connect to a Virtual Desktop Infrastructure to access virtual desktops running Windows 8.1 Enterprise and Office Professional Plus 2013. The users need to access their virtual desktops from their personal devices at home as well. What licenses should they purchase for the 850 PCs? Choose two answers.

    a) Windows 8.1 Enterprise
    b) Windows 8.1 Enterprise + SA
    c) Office Professional Plus 2013
    d) Office Professional Plus 2013 + SA

15. The IT Manager at the Raspberry Rubicon has decided to deploy Exchange Server 2013 Enterprise and has assigned licenses to four servers. How many virtual machines is he licensed to run Exchange Server in on each of the physical servers?

    a) 1
    b) 2
    c) 4
    d) Unlimited

16. Tangerine Truckers are interested in deploying Office 365 for their users. They have identified that users need access to Exchange and SharePoint, as well as Office installed on their devices. They are not intending to deploy Lync since they have a third party solution that they are happy with. What Office 365 USLs should they purchase?

    a) Plan K1 and Office 365 ProPlus
    b) Plan E1
    c) Plan E3
    d) Plan E4

14. World of Magnolia have 850 PCs that connect to a Virtual Desktop Infrastructure to access virtual desktops running Windows 8.1 Enterprise and Office Professional Plus 2013. The users need to access their virtual desktops from their personal devices at home as well. What licenses should they purchase for the 850 PCs? Choose two answers.

    a) Windows 8.1 Enterprise
    b) **Windows 8.1 Enterprise + SA** ✓
    c) Office Professional Plus 2013
    d) **Office Professional Plus 2013 + SA** ✓

15. The IT Manager at the Raspberry Rubicon has decided to deploy Exchange Server 2013 Enterprise and has assigned licenses to four servers. How many virtual machines is he licensed to run Exchange Server in on each of the physical servers?

    a) **1** ✓
    b) 2
    c) 4
    d) Unlimited

16. Tangerine Truckers are interested in deploying Office 365 for their users. They have identified that users need access to Exchange and SharePoint, as well as Office installed on their devices. They are not intending to deploy Lync since they have a third party solution that they are happy with. What Office 365 USLs should they purchase?

    a) Plan K1 and Office 365 ProPlus
    b) Plan E1
    c) **Plan E3** ✓
    d) Plan E4

Questions 17 – 19

17. Vermilion Jewellers have 495 PCs which are licensed with Office Professional Plus 2013. 25 users also want Visio 2013 and Project 2013 installed on their machines. How many additional licenses should Vermilion Jewellers purchase?

   a) No licenses – Visio and Project are part of Office Professional Plus 2013
   b) 25 Visio licenses and 25 Project licenses
   c) 25 Project licenses and no Visio licenses since it's part of Office Professional Plus 2013
   d) 495 Visio licenses and 495 Project licenses

18. Cerise Estate Management have identified that their users need to use Word, Excel, Outlook and Lync. Which edition of Office 2013 would you recommend?

   a) Office Standard 2013
   b) Office Professional 2013
   c) Office Professional Plus 2013
   d) Office Enterprise 2013

19. The IT Manager at Pastel Pink Personal Coaches wants to add Software Assurance to his Windows 8.1 licenses. Which of the following may he add SA to?

   a) Windows 8.1 Pro OEM licenses within 90 days
   b) Windows 8.1 Enterprise OEM licenses within 90 days
   c) Windows 8.1 Pro Volume Licensing licenses at time of purchase
   d) Windows 8.1 Enterprise Volume Licensing licenses at time of purchase

17. Vermilion Jewellers have 495 PCs which are licensed with Office Professional Plus 2013. 25 users also want Visio 2013 and Project 2013 installed on their machines. How many additional licenses should Vermilion Jewellers purchase?

    a) No licenses – Visio and Project are part of Office Professional Plus 2013

    b) 25 Visio licenses and 25 Project licenses ✓

    c) 25 Project licenses and no Visio licenses since it's part of Office Professional Plus 2013

    d) 495 Visio licenses and 495 Project licenses

18. Cerise Estate Management have identified that their users need to use Word, Excel, Outlook and Lync. Which edition of Office 2013 would you recommend?

    a) Office Standard 2013

    b) Office Professional 2013

    c) Office Professional Plus 2013 ✓

    d) Office Enterprise 2013

19. The IT Manager at Pastel Pink Personal Coaches wants to add Software Assurance to his Windows 8.1 licenses. Which of the following may he add SA to?

    a) Windows 8.1 Pro OEM licenses within 90 days

    b) Windows 8.1 Enterprise OEM licenses within 90 days

    c) Windows 8.1 Pro Volume Licensing licenses at time of purchase

    d) Windows 8.1 Enterprise Volume Licensing licenses at time of purchase ✓

Questions 20 – 22

20. The IT staff at Purple Paint Pot Decorators are intending to deploy CRM Server 2013 on a single server for a number of external users to access. They have assigned CRM, Windows Server and SQL Server licenses to the machine. What other license should they assign to the server to allow for external access?

   a) SQL Server 2014 External Connector license
   b) CRM 2013 External Connector license
   c) Windows Server 2012 External Connector license
   d) SharePoint 2013 for Internet Sites license

21. Maroon Balloons have a SQL Server 2014 solution accessed by 275 internal users and over 100 external users. They have opted to deploy the Standard edition of SQL Server 2014. How should they license it?

   a) With Server and CAL licenses for internal users and an External Connector license for external users
   b) With Server and CAL licenses for internal and external users
   c) With Core licenses to cover both internal and external users
   d) With Processor licenses to cover both internal and external users

22. Myrtle Beachwear have deployed Windows Server 2012 R2 and have licensed their estate with a mixture of User and Device CALs. Are they compliant?

   a) Yes, as long as every user and device is covered by one CAL or another, it's OK to mix them
   b) Yes, as long as the total number of CALs is greater than the number of users
   c) No, they need to choose either User or Device CALs
   d) No, Device CALs are not available for Windows Server 2012 R2

Answers 20 – 22

20. The IT staff at Purple Paint Pot Decorators are intending to deploy CRM Server 2013 on a single server for a number of external users to access. They have assigned CRM, Windows Server and SQL Server licenses to the machine. What other license should they assign to the server to allow for external access?

    a) SQL Server 2014 External Connector license
    b) CRM 2013 External Connector license
    c) Windows Server 2012 External Connector license ✓
    d) SharePoint 2013 for Internet Sites license

21. Maroon Balloons have a SQL Server 2014 solution accessed by 275 internal users and over 100 external users. They have opted to deploy the Standard edition of SQL Server 2014. How should they license it?

    a) With Server and CAL licenses for internal users and an External Connector license for external users
    b) With Server and CAL licenses for internal and external users
    c) With Core licenses to cover both internal and external users ✓
    d) With Processor licenses to cover both internal and external users

22. Myrtle Beachwear have deployed Windows Server 2012 R2 and have licensed their estate with a mixture of User and Device CALs. Are they compliant?

    a) Yes, as long as every user and device is covered by one CAL or another, it's OK to mix them ✓
    b) Yes, as long as the total number of CALs is greater than the number of users
    c) No, they need to choose either User or Device CALs
    d) No, Device CALs are not available for Windows Server 2012 R2

Questions 23 – 25

23. Scarlet Key Cutters are about to deploy Project Server 2013 in their organization. What other products are required as part of the technology infrastructure? Choose three answers.

   a) Windows Server
   b) SQL Server
   c) Exchange Server
   d) SharePoint Server
   e) CRM Server

24. Peach Snaps Cameras have purchased four servers and want to deploy SQL Server 2014 Standard edition on all of them. All of the servers have two Intel based processors with eight cores each. How many licenses should they purchase for all of the servers?

   a) 4
   b) 8
   c) 16
   d) 64

25. Spring Green Grocers have deployed Windows Server 2008 R2 and have licensed all 270 users with Windows Server 2008 CALs. They want to deploy another server with Windows Server 2012 R2 installed. All users will be able to access this server, but in reality, only 30 will do so. What additional licenses should they purchase to cover this scenario?

   a) None – their Windows Server 2008 CALs will cover them for Windows Server 2012 R2
   b) 30 Windows Server 2012 CALs
   c) 270 Windows Server 2012 CALs
   d) 300 Windows Server 2012 CALs

Answers 23 – 25

23. Scarlet Key Cutters are about to deploy Project Server 2013 in their organization. What other products are required as part of the technology infrastructure? Choose three answers.

    a) **Windows Server** ✓
    b) **SQL Server** ✓
    c) Exchange Server
    d) **SharePoint Server** ✓
    e) CRM Server

24. Peach Snaps Cameras have purchased four servers and want to deploy SQL Server 2014 Standard edition on all of them. All of the servers have two Intel based processors with eight cores each. How many licenses should they purchase for all of the servers?

    a) 4
    b) 8
    c) 16
    d) **64** ✓

25. Spring Green Grocers have deployed Windows Server 2008 R2 and have licensed all 270 users with Windows Server 2008 CALs. They want to deploy another server with Windows Server 2012 R2 installed. All users will be able to access this server, but in reality, only 30 will do so. What additional licenses should they purchase to cover this scenario?

    a) None – their Windows Server 2008 CALs will cover them for Windows Server 2012 R2
    b) 30 Windows Server 2012 CALs
    c) **270 Windows Server 2012 CALs** ✓
    d) 300 Windows Server 2012 CALs

Questions 26 – 28

26. The senior management team at Coff E-Learning Solutions are worried that their employees cannot find corporate information efficiently enough and have decided that a company portal would assist. What product is likely to meet their needs best for this project?
    a) InfoPath
    b) SharePoint Server
    c) SQL Server
    d) SharePoint Portal Server

27. Mauve Stoves have bought 25 PCs with Windows 8.1 Pro pre-installed. What downgrade rights do they have? Choose two answers.
    a) Windows Vista Business
    b) Windows 7 Professional
    c) Windows 7 Enterprise
    d) Windows 8 Pro
    e) Windows Vista Pro

28. Xanthic Tractors need to give access to their server infrastructure to about 127 external users. They have licensed Windows Server 2012 R2 Datacenter edition with Processor-based licenses and CALs to cover their internal users. How should they license these external users?
    a) With External Connector Processor licenses assigned to the processors in every server
    b) With a single External Connector license per server
    c) With User CALs
    d) With a Datacenter External User Add-on license per server

26. The senior management team at Coff E-Learning Solutions are worried that their employees cannot find corporate information efficiently enough and have decided that a company portal would assist. What product is likely to meet their needs best for this project?

    a) InfoPath
    b) **SharePoint Server** ✓
    c) SQL Server
    d) SharePoint Portal Server

27. Mauve Stoves have bought 25 PCs with Windows 8.1 Pro pre-installed. What downgrade rights do they have? Choose two answers.

    a) **Windows Vista Business** ✓
    b) **Windows 7 Professional** ✓
    c) Windows 7 Enterprise
    d) Windows 8 Pro
    e) Windows Vista Pro

28. Xanthic Tractors need to give access to their server infrastructure to about 127 external users. They have licensed Windows Server 2012 R2 Datacenter edition with Processor-based licenses and CALs to cover their internal users. How should they license these external users?

    a) With External Connector Processor licenses assigned to the processors in every server
    b) **With a single External Connector license per server** ✓
    c) With User CALs
    d) With a Datacenter External User Add-on license per server

Questions 29 – 31

29. The Jazzberry Jam Shop want to acquire licenses for Windows Server 2012 R2 and System Center 2012 R2 for around half of the servers in their server farm which is not virtualized at all. What should they acquire?

   a) Windows Server 2012 R2 Standard and System Center 2012 R2 Standard
   b) Windows Server 2012 R2 Datacenter and System Center 2012 R2 Datacenter
   c) Core Infrastructure Server Suite Standard
   d) Core Infrastructure Server Suite Datacenter

30. Honeydew Hatters need a tool that delivers content management, document collaboration, web conferencing, and enterprise telephony. Which of these will Lync Server 2013 deliver for them? Choose two answers.

   a) Content management
   b) Document collaboration
   c) Web conferencing
   d) Enterprise telephony

31. Amaranth Antiques have licensed all of their devices for Windows 8.1 Enterprise, Office Professional Plus 2013 and the Core CAL Suite. All licenses include Software Assurance. What other licenses should they acquire for these devices to access VDI desktops running Windows 8.1 Enterprise and Office Professional Plus 2013?

   a) Windows VDA license
   b) Windows Server 2012 CAL
   c) Remote Desktop Services 2012 CAL
   d) VDI Suite license

29. The Jazzberry Jam Shop want to acquire licenses for Windows Server 2012 R2 and System Center 2012 R2 for around half of the servers in their server farm which is not virtualized at all. What should they acquire?

    a) Windows Server 2012 R2 Standard and System Center 2012 R2 Standard

    b) Windows Server 2012 R2 Datacenter and System Center 2012 R2 Datacenter

    c) **Core Infrastructure Server Suite Standard** ✓

    d) Core Infrastructure Server Suite Datacenter

30. Honeydew Hatters need a tool that delivers content management, document collaboration, web conferencing, and enterprise telephony. Which of these will Lync Server 2013 deliver for them? Choose two answers.

    a) Content management

    b) Document collaboration

    c) **Web conferencing** ✓

    d) **Enterprise telephony** ✓

31. Amaranth Antiques have licensed all of their devices for Windows 8.1 Enterprise, Office Professional Plus 2013 and the Core CAL Suite. All licenses include Software Assurance. What other licenses should they acquire for these devices to access VDI desktops running Windows 8.1 Enterprise and Office Professional Plus 2013?

    a) Windows VDA license

    b) Windows Server 2012 CAL

    c) **Remote Desktop Services 2012 CAL** ✓

    d) VDI Suite license

Questions 32 – 34

32. The Yellow Soup Tureen is about to deploy Windows Server 2012 R2 but is uncertain of the edition to deploy. Based on the fact that they are unlikely to deploy any virtual servers, which is likely to be the best recommendation for them?

    a) Standard edition
    b) Enterprise edition
    c) Datacenter edition
    d) Physical-Only edition

33. Powderblue Pottery have deployed Lync Server 2013 and all users will make extensive use of the functionality. What CALs should Powderblue Pottery buy for their users? Choose three answers.

    a) Standard CALs
    b) Enterprise CALs
    c) Plus CALs
    d) Voice CALs
    e) Telephony CALs

34. Charcoal Chimney Sweeps have deployed Project Server 2013 to manage some of their large commercial contracts. They need to give access to 125 external users. How should they license these external users?

    a) The Project Server 2013 license covers an unlimited number of external users
    b) With a Project Server 2013 External Connector license
    c) With Project Server 2013 User CALs
    d) With Project Lite USLs

32. The Yellow Soup Tureen is about to deploy Windows Server 2012 R2 but is uncertain of the edition to deploy. Based on the fact that they are unlikely to deploy any virtual servers, which is likely to be the best recommendation for them?

    a) Standard edition ✓
    b) Enterprise edition
    c) Datacenter edition
    d) Physical-Only edition

33. Powderblue Pottery have deployed Lync Server 2013 and all users will make extensive use of the functionality. What CALs should Powderblue Pottery buy for their users? Choose three answers.

    a) Standard CALs ✓
    b) Enterprise CALs ✓
    c) Plus CALs ✓
    d) Voice CALs
    e) Telephony CALs

34. Charcoal Chimney Sweeps have deployed Project Server 2013 to manage some of their large commercial contracts. They need to give access to 125 external users. How should they license these external users?

    a) The Project Server 2013 license covers an unlimited number of external users
    b) With a Project Server 2013 External Connector license
    c) With Project Server 2013 User CALs ✓
    d) With Project Lite USLs

Questions 35 – 37

35. The IT Manager at Copper Feel Fabrics wants to license CRM Online for some users for full sales, service and marketing use. What USLs should he purchase?

    a) Basic USLs
    b) Essential USLs
    c) Full USLs
    d) Professional USLs

36. The Bondi Blue Bistro is a large international chain of restaurants which has deployed Exchange Server 2013 to give their 15,000 staff access to basic email functionality. What licenses should they purchase? Choose two answers.

    a) Exchange Server 2013 Standard Server licenses
    b) Exchange Server 2013 Enterprise Server licenses
    c) Exchange Server 2013 Standard CALs
    d) Exchange Server 2013 Enterprise CALs

37. Fandango Fitness are interested in deploying Windows Server virtual machines in Azure. Which of the following statements are true? Choose three answers.

    a) Windows Server virtual machines are licensed with Windows Server USLs
    b) Windows Server virtual machines are charged at an hourly rate
    c) Windows Server virtual machines are an all-inclusive cost including the price of the Windows Server license and user access
    d) If a Windows Server virtual machine is not running there are no charges
    e) A customer can assign an existing Windows Server license to an empty Azure virtual machine

35. The IT Manager at Copper Feel Fabrics wants to license CRM Online for some users for full sales, service and marketing use. What USLs should he purchase?

    a) Basic USLs
    b) Essential USLs
    c) Full USLs
    d) **Professional USLs** ✓

36. The Bondi Blue Bistro is a large international chain of restaurants which has deployed Exchange Server 2013 to give their 15,000 staff access to basic email functionality. What licenses should they purchase? Choose two answers.

    a) Exchange Server 2013 Standard Server licenses
    b) **Exchange Server 2013 Enterprise Server licenses** ✓
    c) **Exchange Server 2013 Standard CALs** ✓
    d) Exchange Server 2013 Enterprise CALs

37. Fandango Fitness are interested in deploying Windows Server virtual machines in Azure. Which of the following statements are true? Choose three answers.

    a) Windows Server virtual machines are licensed with Windows Server USLs
    b) **Windows Server virtual machines are charged at an hourly rate** ✓
    c) **Windows Server virtual machines are an all-inclusive cost including the price of the Windows Server license and user access** ✓
    d) **If a Windows Server virtual machine is not running there are no charges** ✓
    e) A customer can assign an existing Windows Server license to an empty Azure virtual machine

Questions 38 – 40

38. Goldfinger Food have deployed Windows Server 2012 R2, Exchange Server 2013, SharePoint Server 2013 and SQL Server 2014. They now need to acquire CALs for all their users to access these products for basic use. How would you recommend that they do this in the most cost-effective way?

a) Buy the Core CAL Suite for all users
b) Buy the Enterprise CAL Suite for all users
c) Buy the Core CAL Suite and SQL CALs for all users
d) Buy the Enterprise CAL Suite and SQL CALs for all users

39. The Olive Oil Drum Company have licensed all of their users with the Core CAL Suite. 75 of these users have been given a corporate-owned iPad through which they will access a VDI desktop running Windows 8.1 Enterprise and Office Professional Plus 2013. What additional licenses must they purchase? Choose three answers.

a) Windows 8.1 Enterprise + SA
b) Windows VDA license
c) Office Professional Plus 2013
d) Remote Desktop Services CAL
e) Windows Server CAL

40. Aisle of White Paints have an existing Enterprise Agreement with the Core CAL Suite licensed by Device. They want to extend their identity and access management to the cloud and have improved mobile device management. What licenses should they acquire?

a) The Enterprise Mobility Suite Add-on USL
b) The Enterprise CAL Suite
c) The Azure Rights Management Services USL
d) The Enterprise Mobility Suite Full USL

38. Goldfinger Food have deployed Windows Server 2012 R2, Exchange Server 2013, SharePoint Server 2013 and SQL Server 2014. They now need to acquire CALs for all their users to access these products for basic use. How would you recommend that they do this in the most cost-effective way?

    a) Buy the Core CAL Suite for all users
    b) Buy the Enterprise CAL Suite for all users
    c) **Buy the Core CAL Suite and SQL CALs for all users** ✓
    d) Buy the Enterprise CAL Suite and SQL CALs for all users

39. The Olive Oil Drum Company have licensed all of their users with the Core CAL Suite. 75 of these users have been given a corporate-owned iPad through which they will access a VDI desktop running Windows 8.1 Enterprise and Office Professional Plus 2013. What additional licenses must they purchase? Choose three answers.

    a) Windows 8.1 Enterprise + SA
    b) **Windows VDA license** ✓
    c) **Office Professional Plus 2013** ✓
    d) **Remote Desktop Services CAL** ✓
    e) Windows Server CAL

40. Aisle of White Paints have an existing Enterprise Agreement with the Core CAL Suite licensed by Device. They want to extend their identity and access management to the cloud and have improved mobile device management. What licenses should they acquire?

    a) **The Enterprise Mobility Suite Add-on USL** ✓
    b) The Enterprise CAL Suite
    c) The Azure Rights Management Services USL
    d) The Enterprise Mobility Suite Full USL

Questions 41 – 43

41. Sienna Blenders are intending to run Office 2013 on a server and then to have their users remotely access it using Remote Desktop Services. How would you recommend that Sienna Blenders purchase their Office licenses?

    a) Either via OEM or a Volume Licensing program
    b) Only through OEM
    c) Only through a Volume Licensing program
    d) It does not matter – the use rights for Office do not vary dependent on how a customer acquires the licenses

42. The IT Manager at Lightshades of Grey has mapped out his new server farm infrastructure. He will have five identical AMD servers each with a single processor with six cores and wants SQL Server 2014 Standard to run on each machine, licensed with the Core licensing model. What should he order to cover all of these servers?

    a) 13 x SQL Server 2014 Standard Core 2-packs
    b) 15 x SQL Server 2014 Standard Core 2-packs
    c) 25 x SQL Server 2014 Standard Core licenses
    d) 30 x SQL Server 2014 Standard Core licenses

43. The person in charge of buying software at The Mala Kite Shop wants to buy Office 2013 licenses through a Volume Licensing program that includes Access 2013. Which edition of Office 2013 should he buy?

    a) Office Standard 2013
    b) Office Professional 2013
    c) Office Professional Plus 2013
    d) Office Enterprise 2013

Answers 41 – 43

41. Sienna Blenders are intending to run Office 2013 on a server and then to have their users remotely access it using Remote Desktop Services. How would you recommend that Sienna Blenders purchase their Office licenses?

    a) Either via OEM or a Volume Licensing program
    b) Only through OEM
    c) Only through a Volume Licensing program ✓
    d) It does not matter – the use rights for Office do not vary dependent on how a customer acquires the licenses

42. The IT Manager at Lightshades of Grey has mapped out his new server farm infrastructure. He will have five identical AMD servers each with a single processor with six cores and wants SQL Server 2014 Standard to run on each machine, licensed with the Core licensing model. What should he order to cover all of these servers?

    a) 13 x SQL Server 2014 Standard Core 2-packs ✓
    b) 15 x SQL Server 2014 Standard Core 2-packs
    c) 25 x SQL Server 2014 Standard Core licenses
    d) 30 x SQL Server 2014 Standard Core licenses

43. The person in charge of buying software at The Mala Kite Shop wants to buy Office 2013 licenses through a Volume Licensing program that includes Access 2013. Which edition of Office 2013 should he buy?

    a) Office Standard 2013
    b) Office Professional 2013
    c) Office Professional Plus 2013 ✓
    d) Office Enterprise 2013

Questions 44 – 46

44. Which of the following are benefits of an Office 2013 license purchased through a Volume Licensing program? Choose two answers.

   a) It is perpetual
   b) It gives rights for Office to be installed on a server and accessed through technology such as Remote Desktop Services
   c) It gives rights for the Office components to be split across several devices as required
   d) It gives rights for Office to be installed on a portable device in addition to a main device

45. Which of the following products require SQL Server as part of their infrastructure? Choose three answers.

   a) Windows Server 2012 R2
   b) System Center 2012 R2
   c) SharePoint Server 2013
   d) CRM Server 2013
   e) Exchange Server 2013

46. The Pink Pillow Shop have implemented a Bring Your Own Device policy which means that users are allowed to bring their own devices from home to access their VDI desktops at work if they want to. All of the users at the Pink Pillow Shop are the primary users of devices licensed with Windows 8.1 Enterprise + SA and all users have been assigned an Office 365 E3 USL. What additional licenses should the Pink Pillow Shop acquire for users to access these Windows 8.1 Enterprise/Office Professional Plus 2013 virtual desktops from their personal devices? Choose three answers.

   a) Office Professional Plus 2013 + SA
   b) Remote Desktop Services 2012 User CAL
   c) Windows Server 2012 User CAL
   d) Windows Companion Subscription License
   e) Windows VDA license

44. Which of the following are benefits of an Office 2013 license purchased through a Volume Licensing program? Choose two answers.

    a) It is perpetual
    b) **It gives rights for Office to be installed on a server and accessed through technology such as Remote Desktop Services** ✓
    c) It gives rights for the Office components to be split across several devices as required
    d) **It gives rights for Office to be installed on a portable device in addition to a main device** ✓

45. Which of the following products require SQL Server as part of their infrastructure? Choose three answers.

    a) Windows Server 2012 R2
    b) **System Center 2012 R2** ✓
    c) **SharePoint Server 2013** ✓
    d) **CRM Server 2013** ✓
    e) Exchange Server 2013

46. The Pink Pillow Shop have implemented a Bring Your Own Device policy which means that users are allowed to bring their own devices from home to access their VDI desktops at work if they want to. All of the users at the Pink Pillow Shop are the primary users of devices licensed with Windows 8.1 Enterprise + SA and all users have been assigned an Office 365 E3 USL. What additional licenses should the Pink Pillow Shop acquire for users to access these Windows 8.1 Enterprise/Office Professional Plus 2013 virtual desktops from their personal devices? Choose three answers.

    a) Office Professional Plus 2013 + SA
    b) **Remote Desktop Services 2012 User CAL** ✓
    c) **Windows Server 2012 User CAL** ✓
    d) **Windows Companion Subscription License** ✓
    e) Windows VDA license

Questions 47 – 49

47. The Lemon Launderette are about to upgrade all of their desktop operating systems to Windows 8.1 Pro by buying licenses through a Volume Licensing agreement. They have identified that their existing estate is running the following operating systems currently: Windows Vista Enterprise, Windows Vista Ultimate, Windows 7 Professional, and Windows 7 Home Premium. Which of these is not an eligible qualifying operating system for the Volume Licensing licenses?
   a) Windows Vista Enterprise
   b) Windows Vista Ultimate
   c) Windows 7 Professional
   d) Windows 7 Home Premium

48. Blacken White Solicitors have deployed CRM Server 2013 and bought Basic CALs for 75 of their users. After six months they realize that eight of these users need access to the services of CRM Server licensed by the Professional CAL. What should they do to license this?
   a) Buy Professional Use Additive CALs for the eight users
   b) Buy Basic to Professional Step Up CALs for the eight users
   c) At Anniversary, reduce the number of Basic CALs by 8, and add 8 Professional CALs
   d) Buy 8 Professional CALs and reassign the unused Basic CALs as new users join the organization

49. Mellow Yellow Sounds want their store staff to have access to the company intranet and basic email functionality. They will also need to view and occasionally edit Office documents. How would you recommend they license the users most cost-effectively?
   a) With Office 365 E1 USLs
   b) With Office 365 K1 USLs
   c) With Office Online USLs and Core CAL Suite licenses
   d) With Office Online and K1 USLs

47. The Lemon Launderette are about to upgrade all of their desktop operating systems to Windows 8.1 Pro by buying licenses through a Volume Licensing agreement. They have identified that their existing estate is running the following operating systems currently: Windows Vista Enterprise, Windows Vista Ultimate, Windows 7 Professional, and Windows 7 Home Premium. Which of these is not an eligible qualifying operating system for the Volume Licensing licenses?

    a) Windows Vista Enterprise
    b) Windows Vista Ultimate
    c) Windows 7 Professional
    d) **Windows 7 Home Premium** ✓

48. Blacken White Solicitors have deployed CRM Server 2013 and bought Basic CALs for 75 of their users. After six months they realize that eight of these users need access to the services of CRM Server licensed by the Professional CAL. What should they do to license this?

    a) **Buy Professional Use Additive CALs for the eight users** ✓
    b) Buy Basic to Professional Step Up CALs for the eight users
    c) At Anniversary, reduce the number of Basic CALs by 8, and add 8 Professional CALs
    d) Buy 8 Professional CALs and reassign the unused Basic CALs as new users join the organization

49. Mellow Yellow Sounds want their store staff to have access to the company intranet and basic email functionality. They will also need to view and occasionally edit Office documents. How would you recommend they license the users most cost-effectively?

    a) With Office 365 E1 USLs
    b) **With Office 365 K1 USLs** ✓
    c) With Office Online USLs and Core CAL Suite licenses
    d) With Office Online and K1 USLs

Questions 50 – 53

50. Ochre Poker want to purchase the Enterprise Mobility Suite Add-on USL. Which of the following are qualifying underlying licenses for this Add-on USL? Choose two answers.
    a) Windows 8.1 Enterprise with SA
    b) Core CAL Suite with SA
    c) Windows Intune USL
    d) Enterprise CAL Suite with SA

51. Which of the following licenses are included in the Enterprise CAL Suite? Choose two answers.
    a) Windows AD RMS CAL
    b) Windows RDS CAL
    c) System Center Client Management Suite CML
    d) Lync Plus CAL
    e) SQL CAL

52. Turquoise Toys want to license their users to be able to set-up web conferences using an online service. What is the most cost-effective way for them to license this?
    a) Lync Online Plan 1
    b) Lync Online Plan 2
    c) Office 365 Plan E1
    d) Office 365 Plan K1

53. The IT manager at Taupe Telecoms has a single processor server with four virtual machines running on it. How many System Center 2012 R2 licenses should he assign to the server to manage the virtual machines?
    a) 1
    b) 2
    c) 4
    d) He should assign System Center 2012 R2 Datacenter licenses

50. Ochre Poker want to purchase the Enterprise Mobility Suite Add-on USL. Which of the following are qualifying underlying licenses for this Add-on USL? Choose two answers.

    a) Windows 8.1 Enterprise with SA
    b) **Core CAL Suite with SA** ✓
    c) Windows Intune USL
    d) **Enterprise CAL Suite with SA** ✓

51. Which of the following licenses are included in the Enterprise CAL Suite? Choose two answers.

    a) **Windows AD RMS CAL** ✓
    b) Windows RDS CAL
    c) **System Center Client Management Suite CML** ✓
    d) Lync Plus CAL
    e) SQL CAL

52. Turquoise Toys want to license their users to be able to set-up web conferences using an online service. What is the most cost-effective way for them to license this?

    a) Lync Online Plan 1
    b) **Lync Online Plan 2** ✓
    c) Office 365 Plan E1
    d) Office 365 Plan K1

53. The IT manager at Taupe Telecoms has a single processor server with four virtual machines running on it. How many System Center 2012 R2 licenses should he assign to the server to manage the virtual machines?

    a) 1
    b) **2** ✓
    c) 4
    d) He should assign System Center 2012 R2 Datacenter licenses

PART 3: THE MICROSOFT LICENSING AGREEMENTS

For the exam, you need to be able to recommend the right licensing agreement for the organizations that are described. You need to be confident with, for example, the types of licenses that they allow customers to buy, whether they require a commitment, as well as specifics such as whether Software Assurance is included.

The diagram below gives you a summary of all of the licensing programs that you need to know about for the exam. Here you can see whether the programs require that a larger number of licenses are purchased (the bottom row) or a smaller number (the top row). You can also see which programs require a commitment (the right hand column) or allow customers to buy what they need when they need it, on a transactional basis (the left hand column). The little servers and clouds indicate whether on-premises licenses and/or Online Services can be purchased through a particular agreement, and the SA icons indicate whether Software Assurance is included or an optional purchase.

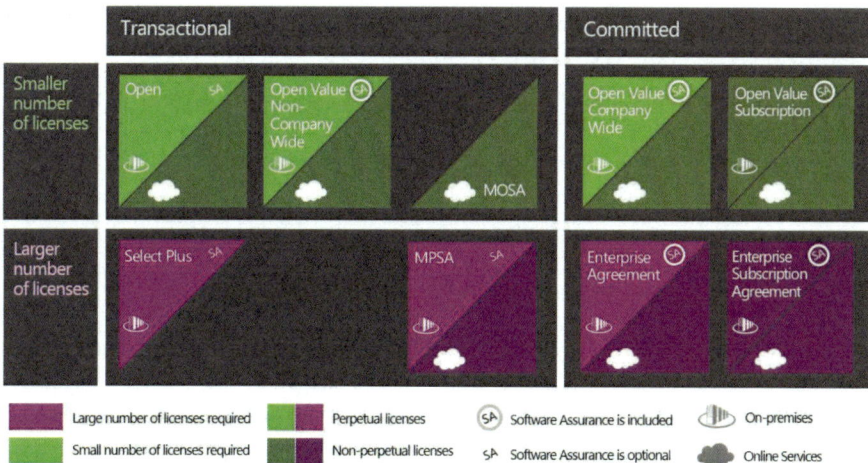

Figure 28: Microsoft Volume Licensing Programs

In July 2014 it was announced that Select Plus would be retiring and you can see from the diagram that the MPSA (Microsoft Products and Services Agreement) is well placed to be its successor since it allows the same transactional flexibility for on-premises licenses but also allows a customer to purchase Online Services through the same agreement.

The Server and Cloud Enrollment is also relatively new – it was launched in 2013 – and it's part of the Enterprise Agreement shown on the diagram.

The exam focusses on commercial customers so, although many of these programs are available for academic or government customers, you don't need to know any detail about these specific programs.

If you already have a good knowledge of the Microsoft Volume Licensing Agreements, why not skip to the Recap Questions on page 176 and test yourself?

Why Volume Licensing?

As we've said, the exam focuses on making sure that you can recommend the right licensing agreement for a customer, and as well as being able to choose the right agreement type, you need to be confident in why Volume Licensing is (generally, and almost always in the exam) a better recommendation for a large organization than buying licenses through FPP or OEM.

As we stated right at the beginning of this book, a license gives you the basic rights to install and use the software, but additional rights are often available and they differ according to the channel through which the software has been purchased – through FPP, OEM or Volume Licensing. Part 5 of this book details the resources you should know which state the different rights for each channel.

Let's now take a look at the main differences between the channels and see why Volume Licensing is an attractive way of purchasing software.

Availability

Microsoft has a comprehensive portfolio of software useful to organizations and all of this is available through the Volume Licensing channel. A smaller subset is available through FPP, and a still smaller subset through OEM – typically it's just the Windows client, Windows Server, and Office available through this channel.

Cost

FPP is the most expensive way of purchasing Microsoft software. Note that in real life there are some exceptions to this, but in the simplified world of the exam, you should consider that FPP is not a cost-effective way of purchasing licenses. Licenses purchased through the OEM channel are often the cheapest price point but you pay a different price – not all software is available and many of the other rights we will talk about in this section are not available. Volume Licensing generally gives discounts to customers in that the more they buy, the cheaper the licenses are.

Downgrade Rights

When you buy a license through FPP or OEM you generally buy the rights to install and use a particular version of the software. However, with Volume Licensing you buy a license for the current version of a product and can then install a previous version if that suits your infrastructure better. As an example, you may actually buy a license for Windows Server 2012 R2 Standard since that's the current version, but you can install any previous version – so perhaps Windows Server 2008 R2 Standard or even Windows Server 2003 Standard. We looked at some exceptions to this in the Products licensing section of this book (specifically Windows 8.1 through OEM) but certainly for the purposes of the exam you should take a requirement for downgrade rights to mean that you should recommend that the customer acquire licenses through a Volume Licensing program.

Upgrade Rights

You need to be a little bit careful with Upgrade Rights – they're not strictly speaking a benefit of Volume Licensing – you don't get them as an automatic right as you do with downgrade rights, for example. But you do get them with Software Assurance and SA is only available through Volume Licensing – so for the exam, you should consider that a business requirement for rights to the latest versions of the software is hinting at a recommendation for purchasing licenses through a Volume Licensing program.

License Reassignment Rights

When you buy a license for, say, Office 2013 through the OEM channel, the software is pre-installed on the device and it is said to "live and die" on that machine – in other words you can't transfer Office 2013 to another machine if the urge takes you – or if your original machine needs to be retired. Many FPP products do allow the purchaser to de-install software from one machine and install it on another, but again, for the purposes of the exam, you should consider that a requirement for reassignment of licenses is guiding you to recommend one of the Volume Licensing agreements. The exception to this is the Windows 8.1 Pro license – when it's purchased through Volume Licensing it is tied to the machine to which it is first assigned and can't be moved. Other Volume Licensing licenses generally allow software to be reassigned to another machine every 90 days, if required. This applies to both on-premises software licenses and also to Online Services Subscription Licenses where licenses can be assigned to different users.

Reimaging Rights

These rights allow customers to make an ideal, company-specific image of an installation of a certain piece of software and then to apply that image to lots of devices, rather than having to install from scratch each time and make customized changes on each machine. Reimaging Rights are granted to all Volume Licensing customers and under these rights, customers can reimage OEM or FPP licensed devices using media provided under the Volume Licensing agreement.

License Manageability

The final reason why a Volume Licensing agreement is often an attractive way for business customers to acquire licenses are the benefits in license manageability. If an organization purchases their licenses as Full Packaged Product, then they need to keep just about all of the packaging and receipts or invoices to show as proof of purchase, which is obviously unwieldy and difficult to manage. However, if they purchase licenses through a Volume Licensing agreement then there are dedicated portals that a customer can use to track their license purchases which makes the whole task of Software Asset Management significantly easier.

Applying your knowledge in the exam:

- Look out for business goals which map directly to these rights. An organization that needs flexibility in the versions of the software that they deploy will need downgrade rights, while a business that is interested in standardizing their desktop software will want reimaging rights. Companies that want to minimize the cost of licensing Office 2013 when they replace desktop machines will find reassignment rights useful so that they can re-use their existing Volume Licensing licenses on the new hardware

- You also need to be able to pick out the benefits from a list to justify why a Volume Licensing solution would be best. A requirement for perpetual licenses would NOT be sufficient to recommend a Volume Licensing agreement for example

- Look out for future requirements that state that the organization is intending to replace some or all of their desktop hardware since acquiring the Windows licenses through OEM may well be the best recommendation for them in this case

- Remember the exceptions that apply to Windows 8.1 so that you don't inadvertently choose the wrong answer in the exam by applying general rules to this product: there are no license reassignment rights when you buy Windows 8.1 Pro through Volume Licensing, and there ARE downgrade rights (to the previous two versions) when you buy Windows 8.1 Pro through OEM

Select Plus Agreements

The Basics

The Select Plus agreement is a framework through which customers purchase the licenses that they require. In particular, customers buy perpetual licenses for on-premises products through the Select Plus agreement and this means that they are licensed to use the products that they buy through the agreement for ever – even if they don't renew the agreement. The agreement is considered to be an evergreen agreement since it doesn't need re-signing every three years as an Enterprise Agreement does.

Software Assurance is a completely optional purchase in a Select Plus agreement; on a license by license basis, customers can choose whether or not they buy SA.

Points and Pools

Every product that Microsoft offer is categorized into one of three product pools, and these pools are key to a Select Plus agreement:

- Systems pool (Windows 8.1 and MDOP, for example)
- Applications pool (Office and the Office family products, for example)
- Servers pool (all Server and CAL licenses)

Each product within these pools is assigned a points count and the Microsoft Volume Licensing Product List has an exhaustive list of all the products and how many points they are each worth, both as just a license and also with SA added. This very useful document is refreshed monthly by Microsoft and you can download it from the link below:

http://www.microsoft.com/licensing/products/products.aspx.

When a customer is working out what licenses they need they should split their "shopping list" of products into these three pools since the program minimums and price levels are dependent on each pool, rather than being aggregated across all pools. This means that a customer could be eligible for the best price level in one pool, the lowest in another, and have no agreement at all for the third pool.

Price Levels

Points within a Select Plus agreement are important since they determine a customer's price level. A customer needs to buy licenses totaling at least 500 points in a particular pool each year to be eligible for a Select Plus agreement. This entitles them to Level A – the basic level – pricing. The table below shows the different numbers of points that customers have to reach each year to be eligible for that pricing, with Level D offering the best prices to customers. Do make sure you learn this table of values for the exam!

Points	Price Level
500	A
4,000	B
10,000	C
25,000	D

Figure 29: Select Plus Agreement Price Levels

A question that you probably have in your mind at this point is what happens when a customer fails to reach the required number of points, or indeed even exceeds the points into the next level from one year to the next. Essentially, "re-levelling" takes place so that a customer receives a price level more appropriate to their level of spending (up or down). Note that for the exam you just need to be able to state which price level a customer would be eligible for, rather than being able to solve operational issues when price levels change.

Select Plus agreements are targeted at customers with 250 PCs or more and although the program minimums don't refer to a specific number of PCs, if a customer with 250 PCs bought Office for all of those machines at 2 points per license, this would total 500 points – the program minimum.

Payment

Payment options for Select Plus agreement customers are dependent on whether Software Assurance is purchased with licenses. If licenses are purchased without SA, then a customer must pay the full amount of the license in the month in which the product is installed. These are often called "monthly" payments but don't be misled by imagining that this is the cost of the license split over the term of the agreement and paid in monthly instalments – it's not, it's the single, full payment for the licenses.

If SA is purchased with licenses then customers are eligible to spread the payments for the licenses and SA. As an example, if a customer buys 400 Office licenses with SA at the start of their agreement, they make an initial payment of one third of the license cost and a year's SA, and then repeat that payment at the start of the next two years of the agreement.

Commitment

A customer purchasing through a Select Plus agreement has complete flexibility in the licenses that they purchase; although they need to commit to purchasing 500 points within a particular pool each year, they do not have to buy any specific licenses or to commit to buying Software Assurance at all. This is often called a "transactional" agreement or a "pay as you go" agreement, and is ideal for a customer who wants to buy licenses as projects come up, or sees no particular benefit in, for example, standardizing the software they install on each desktop.

A customer adding Software Assurance to licenses that they purchase through a Select Plus agreement will receive access to a number of SA benefits. However, there are certain benefits that are not available to Select Plus customers unless they make a further level of commitment. If a customer is happy to buy SA on ALL licenses in a particular pool, then they are said to have "Software Assurance Membership", or SAM, for that pool and then gain the maximum number of SA benefits for that pool. Typically, all SA benefits are available to EA customers with fewer available to Select Plus customers. However, adding SAM ensures that the SA benefits for a Select Plus customer are the same as an EA customer.

Affiliates

A key concept to feel comfortable with for the exam is how an organization can work with its affiliates when purchasing licenses. Typically, one organization signs a Microsoft Business and Services Agreement (MBSA). A Select Plus agreement is then set up under the MBSA and one or more affiliates may then purchase licenses through this agreement. There are two main types of affiliates that may purchase under a Select Plus agreement, and these affiliates may be located anywhere in the world:

- Business units, divisions or subsidiaries
- A separate legal entity which owns and controls, is owned and controlled by, or is under common ownership and control with, the organization signing the MBSA, where ownership must be more than 50%

The Select Plus agreement is a great way for a customer and its affiliates to purchase licenses and to take advantage of better price levels through combined purchasing. However, they do still keep complete flexibility in their purchases since each affiliate can buy exactly what they need when they need it, separate to the needs of the other affiliates.

Applying your knowledge in the exam:

- There are many similarities in the Select Plus and MPSA agreements so we'll look at applying your knowledge in the exam for both agreements at the end of the next section

Microsoft Products and Services Agreement (MPSA)

The Basics

The Microsoft Products and Services Agreement was first introduced in December 2013 in the US, UK, Canada and Germany and gradually gained wider availability after that. In July 2014 the retirement of Select Plus was announced and the MPSA is very much positioned to be the replacement for that, and you'll see the similarities between these two transactional programs as we go through the key facts for the MPSA. Be aware of one of the key differences as well though – you can't buy Online Services through Select Plus whereas you can buy both licenses for on-premises products and Online Services through the MPSA.

Purchasing Accounts

One of the key concepts to be familiar with for the MPSA is the notion of Purchasing Accounts. If you understand how affiliates work in Select Plus then the idea is broadly similar but much more useful. Purchasing Accounts allow an organization to structure themselves exactly as they want with regards to purchasing their licenses, but with the advantage of purchasing under a single agreement. This gives rise to two main benefits: that price levels dependent on volume are set across the whole agreement, and that one Purchasing Account is set as the Agreement Administrator which means that they get a consolidated view of all of the assets across the whole organization, and you can imagine how useful this is from a Software Asset Management point of view.

Every organization can set up their Purchasing Accounts in different ways and it's probably a good idea to look at some of the most common scenarios that you'll see, so let's take some fictional companies as examples. Firstly, perhaps Cyan Ida's Pharmacy want to have a centralized purchasing strategy – they could set up a single Purchasing Account through which all licenses are purchased for all departments of the organization to use.

Alternatively, Cerise Estate Management might have a head office and then lots of branch offices that they want to allow to purchase their own licenses. They would set up a Purchasing Account for the head office and then one for each of the branch offices and you can imagine in this scenario that it would probably be the head office that was designated as the Agreement Administrator.

And finally, perhaps Fandango Fitness have a whole host of subsidiaries that they'd like to allow to purchase under a single agreement to get a better price level. This would be possible too under the MPSA as long as the subsidiaries are more than 50% owned.

So, Purchasing Accounts can be set up for either a single legal entity, for divisions within a company, or for separate legal entities that are more than 50% owned by the organization signing the MPSA. All of these approaches may be combined for a single organization if that's the best fit for them. Technically, the MPSA has to be active in the country where a subsidiary is located, so do remember that the MPSA was active in the UK, US, Canada and Germany at the time the exam was written, so that you can correctly choose organizations that could be included in the MPSA.

Each Purchasing Account purchases their licenses through a partner, and they can choose one or more partners to assign to their individual Purchasing Account.

Points and Pools
Points and pools work in exactly the same way as with Select Plus: the products are assigned to exactly the same pools with the same points value and then totaled across an individual pool. However, what is different to a Select Plus agreement is that Online Services are also included in the MPSA and all of these licenses are allocated a points value too. And, as we've said, license purchases from all Purchasing Accounts contribute to the total for a pool.

Price Levels

The price levels are exactly the same as Select Plus but there is an alternative minimum for level A pricing. If a customer is only buying Online Services then they can achieve the minimum for Level A by acquiring 250 USLs.

Payment

Broadly speaking, the payment options are the same as for Select Plus: if you buy licenses without SA then the payment is due in full at the time of software installation, and if you buy licenses with SA then there is the option to spread payments. In Select Plus the license cost is split equally into three and paid at three points in the agreement whereas with the MPSA it's split into different amounts dependent on when the license and SA is purchased. For the exam, you just need to know that both programs support spread payments if SA is purchased with a license, rather than being required to do complicated calculations of any sort!

Commitment

And finally, the commitment levels are the same as for Select Plus – as long as the minimums are met, then an organization doesn't have to buy any particular licenses at any particular times. There is also no commitment to buy Software Assurance but, if required, Software Assurance Membership (SAM) is available under the MPSA and it works in exactly the same way again – you commit to buy SA on all licenses in a particular pool and then get increased SA benefits.

Applying your knowledge in the exam:

- Look carefully at the business goals for an organization – if they want to upgrade just part of their estate or purchase SA on just some of their licenses, then recommend the MPSA or Select Plus rather than the Enterprise Agreements which require licensing commitment across the organization

- If you look at the customer requirements and end up with a choice between Select Plus and the MPSA, always recommend the MPSA, since it allows customers to purchase both Online Services and on-premises licenses which obviously makes the task of license management easier

- You may be asked to state what price level a customer would achieve if they were to sign a new MPSA or Select Plus agreement. You won't be expected to know all the points for individual products, but you should be able to state the relevant price level given the total points for the licenses that they intend to purchase

- Remember that there is a different minimum requirement if a customer is only buying Online Services through the MPSA, so do recommend an MPSA if the customer will only need 250 USLs, rather than being focused completely on the 500 points minimum

- You will need to be able to recommend how an organization could set up their Purchasing Accounts, so make sure that you remember that when an MPSA is signed by an organization they can set up PAs for divisions within the company or for separate legal entities of which they own more than 50%

- Both the MPSA and Select Plus agreements support affiliates on a global level, just remember that the MPSA wasn't active in every geography when the exam was written so you should make sure that any affiliates that you include in your recommendations are based in the UK, US, Canada or Germany

Enterprise and Enterprise Subscription Agreements

The Basics

Enterprise Agreements and Enterprise Subscription Agreements are well named since it's obvious that the difference between them is the word "subscription". Both are Volume Licensing agreements with a three year term, where SA is included, but an Enterprise Agreement enables customers to buy perpetual licenses for on-premises software, and an Enterprise Subscription Agreement is for acquiring non-perpetual licenses. Both types of agreements allow organizations to purchase subscription licenses for Online Services.

As you know, perpetual licenses mean that customers are licensed to use the products that they buy through the agreement for ever – even if they don't renew the agreement.

Non-perpetual licenses – also called subscription licenses – only license software to be used during the term of the agreement, and at the end of the agreement the customer can choose to renew the agreement and carry on using the software, not renew and de-install all software, or buy-out the licenses – that is, convert them to perpetual licenses and use the software for ever, as described above. Non-perpetual licenses are cheaper than perpetual licenses since customers are, in effect, just leasing the software rather than owning it.

I'll use the term "Enterprise Agreement" to refer to both of these agreements throughout this section since many of the program attributes are the same. Where there are differences I'll make sure to highlight these by using terms such as a perpetual Enterprise Agreement or the Enterprise Subscription Agreement.

Enrollments

For a long time the Enterprise Agreement was exclusively based on an Enterprise-Wide Commitment to desktop products. Today, however, a customer can use an EA to commit to either the desktop products or to the server products, and the terms and conditions are contained in something called an Enrollment. There is an Enterprise Enrollment for the desktop products, and a Server and Cloud Enrollment for the server products. Because the Enterprise Enrollment was the only enrollment available under an EA for a long time, for many people it remains synonymous with an EA and in the exam you should consider an EA and the Enterprise Enrollment to mean the same thing, with the Server and Cloud Enrollment being called just that, or the SCE. So, this section will look at how the desktop commitment works, and then a bit later we will look at the SCE.

Enterprise-Wide Commitment
Within the Enterprise Enrollment there is a requirement to standardize the desktop which means that a customer must count up all the "Qualified Devices" in their organization, and then choose an "Enterprise Product" that they are prepared to license for all of these Qualified Devices.

A Qualified Device is any device that can run Windows locally in a physical or virtual operating system environment or one that's used to access a Virtual Desktop Infrastructure. A customer must count all devices as part of their Qualified Device total unless they qualify as one of the following exceptions:

- A PC that is used as a server

- An Industry device – one that only runs hotel booking software, for example

- A device that is not managed by the organization

You need to know the definitions above for the exam but if you would like more detail on how, for example, you determine if a device is actually managed by an organization then there's an excellent Volume Licensing Brief issued by Microsoft that gives a lot more detail.

The Enterprise Products are listed below and for any chosen product, the customer must purchase the same number of licenses as they have Qualified Devices:

- Windows 8.1 Enterprise
- Office Professional Plus 2013
- Core CAL Suite or Enterprise CAL Suite

Note that if a customer chooses to license the CAL Suites by user, then they must count their Qualified Users and buy that number of CAL Suite licenses. Consider, for the purposes of the exam, that a Qualified User is anyone who uses a Qualified Device. If you're curious, or want more detail, you will find the full definitions for both Qualified Users and Qualified Devices in the Enterprise Enrollment document.

Customers who choose a single product enterprise-wide enter into what is known as a "Component EA". If they choose to license all three components – Windows, Office and a CAL Suite – then this is known as a platform, and the customer is said to have a "Platform EA".

Note that in an enterprise-wide agreement there are no portable use rights for Office; a customer cannot choose to count all their desktop machines and then license all their portable machines under the portable use rights. In an enterprise-wide agreement they must count ALL their devices (desktop machines and portable devices) and buy that number of Office licenses.

It's also worth noting that if a company standardizes on Office 2013 through the enterprise-wide agreements then they must purchase Office Professional Plus 2013; if an organization DID want to standardize on Office Standard 2013 then they would need to purchase these licenses through a Select Plus agreement. Some of you may know customers who HAVE standardized on Office Standard 2013 through an EA – Microsoft do often grant exceptions, but you should learn the standard, programmatic elements of the EA for the exam.

Discounts

Because the Enterprise Agreements require a level of customer commitment to standardize on components on the desktop, there are discounts available compared to a Select Plus agreement. For example, if a customer has 500 PCs and chooses to buy Office Professional Plus 2013 licenses with SA for all of them through an EA, then they will receive a significant discount compared to making exactly the same purchase through a Select Plus agreement. In addition, there's a further discount available if the customer signs up for the whole platform in an EA, and of course opting for subscription licenses in an Enterprise Subscription Agreement reduces the cost still further.

Price Levels

There are four different price levels available to an Enterprise Agreement customer, with discounts increasing between the levels. The discounts are based on the number of Qualified Devices or Qualified Users, with Level A requiring that a customer have 250 Qualified Devices/Users to sign the Enterprise Agreement. You should learn the numbers of Qualified Devices/Users for each level for the exam.

Qualified Devices/Users	Price Level
250	A
2,400	B
6,000	C
15,000	D

Figure 30: Enterprise Agreement Price Levels

Additional Products

Customers with an Enterprise Agreement can also choose to license all of the other available products through their agreement and these products (Windows Server, Visio, SQL CALs etc.) are known as Additional Products. Organizations may buy as many, or as few, of these products as they want to, and the number of Additional Products licenses has no bearing on the price level, which is governed solely by the number of Qualified Devices and/or Users.

Payment

Any licenses for products that are on a customer's initial order when they sign the Enterprise Agreement are eligible for spread payments, and this applies to both Enterprise and Additional Products. For a customer with a perpetual EA, they pay a third of the license cost and a year's SA at the start of each year of the agreement. Subscription EA customers actually pay an agreed annual fee for their products at the start of each year, but these are still considered to be spread payments as far as the exam is concerned.

Customers can add licenses at any time for Additional Products that they have not purchased before. A payment must be made in the month of installation, and while this is often known as a monthly payment, remember it's actually a one-off payment in that month rather than a spread monthly option.

True Up and True Down

Customers signing a perpetual Enterprise Agreement do so with a stated number of Qualified Devices/Users. At the first anniversary they count up any new Qualified Devices or Users that may have been added and pay for Enterprise Product licenses for those devices or users during a process known as True Up. This process is then repeated on the second anniversary and at the end of the agreement. Note that while the number of Qualified Devices/Users may go up during the agreement, it is not allowed to decrease. If customers have added licenses for any Additional Products that were on the initial order, then these are trued up in the same way.

Organizations with an Enterprise Subscription Agreement have the flexibility of increasing or decreasing the number of their Qualified Devices/Users as circumstances dictate, and simply declare and pay for the number of devices in use or the number of Qualified Users for the following year at the anniversary. Often, if the number of devices or users goes down this is known as a True Down. Customers may decrease their Qualified Devices/Users at an anniversary as long as they do not decrease below the program minimum of 250 PCs, and you can imagine that organizations with a seasonal business with fluctuating numbers often find this agreement attractive.

Affiliates
Affiliates may also buy under an organization's Enterprise Agreement, although the definition of an affiliate does differ from that in an MPSA or Select Plus agreement. There is only one type of affiliate eligible to purchase under an Enterprise Agreement:

- A separate legal entity which owns and controls, is owned and controlled by, or is under common ownership and control with, the organization signing the MBSA, where ownership must be more than 50%

Affiliate organizations can be located anywhere in the world and, in the same way as the main company, they must commit enterprise-wide to Enterprise Products for all of their Qualified Devices/Users. The Enterprise Agreement gives these organizations a single agreement to buy licenses under, and the price level for the EA is calculated against the total number of Qualified Devices/Users across all affiliates.

Applying your knowledge in the exam:

- Make sure that you know the options that a customer has available to them at the end of an Enterprise Subscription Agreement so that you can choose the right recommendation if their existing agreement is coming to an end. Recommend renewing the agreement if they want to continue the agreement as before, or suggest buying out the licenses if they want to convert them to perpetual licenses. The third option is that they don't renew the agreement and must de-install all their software – an unlikely correct answer in the exam!

- Remember that it is only the Enterprise Subscription Agreement that allows the number of Qualified Devices/Users to go down as well as up, so as soon as the business goals state that an organization needs this flexibility or has a fluctuating number of employees, then this is the agreement to recommend. Also look out for organizations that actively want to decrease licenses or employees through the term of their agreement

- Remember the two restrictions with Office licenses purchased through an enterprise-wide agreement: there are no portable use rights, and the edition purchased must be Office Professional Plus

- Look out for business goals that state that the IT department want to standardize on an enterprise-wide desktop to make deployment and management of the desktops easier, or for problem statements such as an organization having file sharing compatibility issues, since a standardized desktop would be a great recommendation for them

- You may need to calculate the total Qualified Devices for an organization so make sure that you know the exceptions for the devices that don't need to be included: PCs used as a server, industry devices, and devices that aren't managed

- Make sure that you know the Enterprise Products so that you can confidently pick them out of a list and disregard any red herrings such as an organization which has "standardized" by covering all their users with the Windows CAL

- You'll need to be able to determine the relevant price level for a given EA customer. Typically, this will take the form of some business goals which state that the organization wants to expand, so make sure that you read through carefully to count up all the Qualified Devices/Users to choose the right price level

Office 365 in the Enterprise Agreement

For many years the EA has been a vehicle for customers to purchase licenses for on-premises products with the Enterprise-Wide Commitment being made up of Windows, Office, and the CAL Suites. However, with the importance of the cloud, the EA has been updated in recent years to make it easier and more cost-effective for customers to buy Office 365 licenses and, where appropriate, for them to be part of the Enterprise-Wide Commitment. In this section we'll take a look at the different options customers have for buying Office 365 through the Enterprise Agreement.

Adding on Online Services

Let's look first of all at the Office 365 Add-ons. Customers who have existing licenses for either a component or the whole platform EA, keep these licenses – and thus their existing Enterprise-Wide Commitment – but can choose to purchase Add-ons to give access to Office 365 too. As is usual with Add-ons, you need a qualifying license before you can buy an Add-on and in the table below the qualifying licenses are shown in the top row. Then, down the side is the list of Add-ons, and obviously the ticks indicate the eligible combinations.

	Core CAL Suite	Core CAL Suite + Office Professional Plus	Enterprise CAL Suite	Enterprise CAL Suite + Office Professional Plus
E1	✔	✔		
E3		✔		✔
E3 without O365 ProPlus	✔	✔	✔	✔
E4		✔		✔
E4 without O365 ProPlus	✔	✔	✔	✔

Figure 31: Office 365 Add-ons Available in the EA

So you can see that a customer with the Core CAL Suite could purchase the E1 Add-on and in this situation the Core CAL Suite licenses would continue to license the on-premises productivity servers, with the E1 Add-on licensing the equivalent services in the cloud. You can see that there are some Office 365 SKUs that we haven't seen before – E3 and E4 without Office 365 ProPlus and these are the only flavors of E3 and E4 that a CAL Suite-only customer can purchase.

The Add-ons are Additional Products in the EA and that means that there is no particular minimum number of licenses that a customer must buy. There is a maximum however – the number of Add-ons must never exceed the number of underlying qualifying licenses.

As you would expect, these Office 365 Add-on licenses are User Subscription Licenses and in case you were wondering, it's absolutely fine to add a USL on to a qualifying device license.

Transitioning to Online Services
In the previous example, a customer kept the structure of their existing EA and just added on access to Online Services. However, there is an alternative which is to transition to Online Services. Think of a transition as a trading in of licenses – you are swapping paying for your existing on-premises licenses for an Online Services equivalent set of licenses.

Let's take a simple example to start with to see how this works. Imagine that a customer with a Core CAL Suite wants to transition to Office 365 Plan E1. Currently he is paying for six components in the Core CAL Suite and three of those (the productivity servers) will be covered when he moves to E1. However, what about the core infrastructure products – the Windows Server CAL and System Center components? Those products remain installed on-premises and must be licensed, and it's another type of license that is required here – a Bridge CAL. The Bridge CAL licenses all of the other components when the productivity servers licensing is moved to E1.

The table below shows the licenses the customer has before the transition (Core CAL Suite) and the different components that are contained in that license. The After Transition columns show the E1 and Bridge CAL licenses and the positioning indicates the equivalence of the components.

Before Transition	After Transition	
Core CAL Suite	Office 365 Plan E1	Core CAL Bridge for Office 365
Exchange Standard CAL	Exchange Online Plan 1	
SharePoint Standard CAL	SharePoint Online Plan 1	
Lync Standard CAL	Lync Online Plan 2	
Windows Server CAL		Windows Server CAL
SC Config Manager CML		SC Config Manager CML
SC Endpoint Protection SL		SC Endpoint Protection SL

Figure 32: Transitioning Core CAL to E1 and the Bridge

There are a couple of transitions that you should know for the exam. Learn the table below so that you can answer questions where you are given a licensing starting point for the customer and need to pick out the licenses they would have after their transition to the cloud. For example, a customer who has the Professional Desktop Platform would transition to Windows (no change), E3, and the Core CAL Bridge for Office 365:

Existing Licenses	Transition
Core CAL Suite	E1 + Core CAL Bridge for Office 365
Core CAL Suite + Office Professional Plus 2013	E3 + Core CAL Bridge for Office 365
Enterprise CAL Suite + Office Professional Plus 2013	E3 + Enterprise CAL Bridge for Office 365

Figure 33: Office 365 Transitions in the EA

Enterprise Online Services Only EA

And the final part of this section is to let you know about an Enterprise Agreement that breaks all the rules that we've talked about so far! There is a special flavor of the EA called an Enterprise Online Services Only EA which allows a customer to do just that – use the EA framework to buy only Enterprise Online Services. In this type of EA there is no Enterprise-Wide Commitment required.

And which are the Enterprise Online Services? It's easy to remember – the Enterprise Plans, so E1, E3 and E4. A customer can start an EA with 250 USLs of any of the Enterprise Online Services and they can be a combination if required.

Applying your knowledge in the exam:

- Be ready to pick out the Add-ons that a customer would be eligible for so make sure that you learn the table above (Figure 31), taking note that Office Professional Plus 2013 on its own is never a qualifying license for an Add-on

- Remember that an Add-on is an Additional Product so there is no minimum number of licenses that a customer must buy, but there is a maximum – the number of Add-ons can never exceed the number of qualifying licenses

- You won't get any difficult questions on transitions in the exam, but do learn the table above (Figure 33) so that you can answer the questions you do get with confidence

- And remember that while there are lots of rules in place for a "traditional" EA, a customer may also start an EA with just 250 USLs so keep that in mind as a recommendation

Server and Cloud Enrollment

Overview

The Server and Cloud Enrollment (SCE) is the second enrollment that is available to be signed under the Enterprise Agreement. The Enterprise Enrollment covers the desktop products and the SCE focusses on the server products. A customer may choose to have either or both of these Enrollments – they're absolutely not dependent on each other. The SCE does share some characteristics with the Enterprise Enrollment: the term is three years, there's a level of commitment, and Software Assurance is mandatory. If you're familiar with the Enrollment for Application Platform (EAP) or the Enrollment for Core Infrastructure (ECI) then many notions within the SCE will seem familiar since the SCE replaced both the EAP and ECI.

There are four components available under the SCE and the customer chooses the one that corresponds to the licenses that they want to acquire. The table below shows which products are available under which component, the program minimums, and the commitment that is required from the customer:

Components	Application Platform	Core Infrastructure	Developer Tools	Azure
Products	SQL Server + optionally BizTalk and/or SharePoint	Windows Server and System Center	Visual Studio	Microsoft Azure Services
Minimums	**SQL:** 5 Servers and 250 CALs, or 50 Cores **SharePoint:** 5 Servers **BizTalk:** 24 Cores	25 Core Infrastructure Server Suites	20 licenses of Visual Studio Premium and/or Ultimate	$1,200 Annual Monetary Commitment
Commitment	SA on installed base	SA on installed base	SA on installed base	Upfront Monetary Commitment

Figure 34: SCE Components

The Azure component behaves a little differently from the other components and we'll consider that separately at the end of this section. For the other three components, customers get a discount when they buy products through the SCE rather than buying them as Additional Products on an existing EA.

The Price Level of an SCE is set by a qualifying agreement – so if a customer has a Select Plus or Enterprise Agreement in the relevant pool then that Price Level is applied to the SCE. For example, if a customer has a Select Plus agreement at Level B in the servers pool then they would be eligible for Level B pricing when they signed an Application Platform SCE. If there is no qualifying agreement then the SCE is set at Price Level A.

Application Platform Component

As you can see in the table above, the Application Platform component centers around SQL Server. If a customer wants to commit to SQL Server then the SCE is a great mechanism for them to purchase it through. If they are prepared to commit to SQL Server then they can optionally add on SharePoint and/or BizTalk Server too, but do note that they wouldn't be able to sign an SCE with just SharePoint or BizTalk Server.

I think the best way of learning about the SCE is to take some sample customer scenarios so let's first consider Cyan Ida's Pharmacy who have SQL Server 2008 and 2012 and are interested in upgrading their whole estate to SQL Server 2014. This makes them an ideal candidate for the SCE, so how would they go about signing an SCE? The first stage is to document the installed base of SQL Server and Cyan Ida's Pharmacy's current SQL Server estate is shown below:

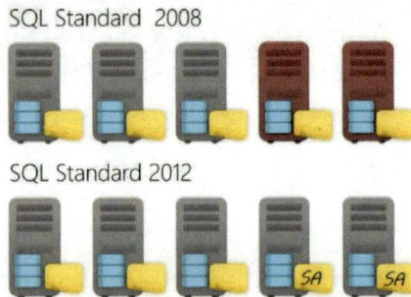

Figure 35: Cyan Ida's Pharmacy – SQL Server Estate

You can see that they have a mixed estate of SQL Server Standard 2008 and 2012 licensed with the Server / CAL model. All of the servers have licenses assigned to them, but only two of the SQL 2012 servers have licenses with active Software Assurance. Two of the SQL 2008 servers (shown in red) are currently running SQL Server but will be retired within the next 18 months.

Once the installed base is calculated, Cyan Ida's Pharmacy must sign their SCE with an initial order which covers this entire base with Software

Assurance. They have a choice of three types of licenses in order to cover each server with SA: either SA renewal, L&SA, or a Subscription license.

They should renew the SA for the two servers with active SA, and then purchase L&SA or Subscription licenses for the other servers. The Subscription licenses are new for the Server and Cloud Enrollment so let's find out a bit more about these now.

There are Subscription licenses available for all of the different SQL Server licenses – so Server licenses, CALs, and Core licenses – and for all of the editions, and purchasing Subscription licenses fulfils the requirement for having active SA on licenses. The Subscription licenses are MSUs – Monthly Subscription Units – which means that they show as a monthly price on the price list which makes for easy pro-rating if a customer adds them part way through an agreement. As you would expect from the name, a customer never owns a Subscription license. Customers may mix and match Subscription licenses with L&SA or SA to cover their entire estate.

Cyan Ida's Pharmacy have a choice of MSUs or L&SA to cover the servers currently without active SA. Which should they choose? Well, price may be a deciding factor for them; if they don't need or want to own perpetual licenses they may decide to move to the Subscription model since these licenses are priced at about 35% of the License price. They have eight servers that they need to cover with SA and buying L&SA for all of them could be too high a cost.

Another reason for buying MSUs is that the number of licenses may be reduced during the term of the agreement. The two red servers indicated that the servers were due to be retired in the next 18 months or so. Because they are currently running SQL Server, they must be included in the agreement and covered with SA, but Cyan Ida's Pharmacy don't need these servers in the long term and so buying L&SA for these servers doesn't make sense if there is a Subscription alternative. As long as they buy 12 months' worth of an MSU they can reduce numbers at the next anniversary.

Cyan Ida's Pharmacy do want to own licenses long-term and so they decide to purchase L&SA for most of the servers and MSUs for the two servers that will be retired. This means that their initial order will consist of 2 x SQL Standard Server SA, 6 x SQL Standard Server L&SA, and 2 x SQL Standard Server MSU. At the first anniversary they decide whether they want to continue with the MSUs – they can decrease the number to zero if they no longer need the servers or pay another 12 months for one or both of the servers depending on their needs.

Note that there's complete flexibility with the SCE – if Cyan Ida's Pharmacy's plans change, they could add more servers and cover them with MSUs part the way through a year. At anniversary they pay for the complete months that the servers were used in the previous year and for 12 months for the following year. Once 12 months have been paid, the MSUs can be reduced again if required. Equally, since Cyan Ida's Pharmacy actually prefer to own licenses, they could add a server and then true-up the L&SA cost at the next anniversary.

Core Infrastructure Component

The Core Infrastructure component is all about Windows Server and System Center which must be purchased together as the Core Infrastructure Server (CIS) Suites. The rules are very similar to the Application Platform component that we've just considered, so let's do what we did before and take another company example.

This time it's the Olive Oil Drum Company who have Windows Server and System Center installed on some servers throughout their estate. They are prepared to license all servers with the CIS Suites and so, again, are an ideal candidate for the SCE. You can see their current installed base below where each server actually represents ten servers:

CIS Standard

Windows Server 2012 R2 Standard

Figure 36: The Olive Oil Drum Company – Windows/System Center Estate

You can see that all servers have licenses assigned to them – some of which have active Software Assurance, and some of which do not. The Olive Oil Drum Company must do exactly what Cyan Ida's Pharmacy did – make an initial order which covers all Windows servers with the CIS Suites with active SA. Again, they have the option to renew SA where there is active SA, and buy L&SA or Subscription licenses where there is not.

Let's take each group of servers separately and see what they should purchase in each case. The top group of servers are currently licensed with the CIS Suite Standard with active SA. Note that there's just a single license assigned to the servers since the licensing model for the CIS Suites is exactly the same as both Windows Server and System Center – one license must be assigned for every two physical processors on the server. So, a single CIS Suite Standard license covers two processors for both Windows Server Standard and System Center Standard. Since the SA is active, the Olive Oil Drum Company would simply purchase CIS Standard SA for these servers in their SCE.

The second group of servers has two servers which have active SA on Windows Server only, and two servers which have no active SA and which are due to be retired in the short term – shown again by the red servers. Let's start with those red servers; they need to be licensed with CIS Suite Standard licenses – one license for each server – and because they're due to be retired shortly it's probably a good idea to license them with CIS Standard Suite MSUs. The Olive Oil Drum Company could alternatively choose L&SA for these servers of course if that suited their business needs better.

The other two servers in this group need to be licensed with CIS Suite Standard licenses too – but are they L&SA or SA licenses? There is active SA on the Windows Server component, but not the System Center one. They can't therefore renew the SA for CIS, but it seems unfair to make them re-purchase the Windows license by forcing them to buy CIS Suite Standard L&SA. The solution to this is a special flavor of the CIS Suites called "CIS Suite Standard without Windows Server L&SA". This, in effect, renews the SA on Windows Server and provides L&SA for the System Center component. There's a Datacenter version of this SKU too, and a "without System Center" version for the exact opposite – when the customer has active SA on System Center but not on Windows Server.

So the initial order for the Olive Oil Drum Company is as follows: 20 x CIS Suite Standard SA, 20 x CIS Suite Standard without Windows Server L&SA, 20 x CIS Suite Standard MSU.

There's just one final thing you need to know about the Core Infrastructure component and that's another benefit that's available specifically for customers who enroll in this component. This benefit is the Cloud Management Benefit and it allows customers to install System Center and manage up to 10 Windows Azure virtual machines for each CIS Suite license that they have purchased.

Developer Tools Component

The Developer Tools component is the last of the three SCE components that all behave in a very similar way. It is, of course, the mechanism for customers to acquire Visual Studio licenses and all of the rules that we've looked at apply to this component too – the installed base must meet the minimum requirements and then all licenses must be covered with SA.

Azure

As I mentioned earlier in this section, Azure is treated slightly differently to the other three components that we've just looked at. If you sign an SCE with any of the three components then you have automatic provisioning of Azure. This means that technically you're ready to use any of the Azure services and you're just invoiced quarterly for whatever you consume. This is ideal for customers who don't really want to make a commitment to Azure but are interested in trying it out.

However, for customers who want the best possible prices on Azure and are prepared to make a commitment, there's the Azure-only SCE which requires an upfront Monetary Commitment to Azure.

A customer estimates at the start of their agreement how much they think they are likely to spend on Azure Services; this is not as random as it sounds – there's a calculator to help with estimating spend and, if you follow some recommendations, there are no penalties for not getting the estimates exactly right. The amount that a customer estimates that they will spend in the year is known as the Annual Monetary Commitment and is paid in full at the beginning of each year of the agreement.

So what happens if the customer doesn't get the Annual Monetary Commitment exactly right and either underspends or overspends in a particular year? Well, the underspend is easy – the customer forfeits the remaining funds at the end of the year. For this reason, you should always recommend that the customer makes an Annual Monetary Commitment for a lesser amount than perhaps they would originally estimate.

For the next example, let's consider the Olive Oil Drum Company in the diagram below. You can see that they made an Annual Monetary Commitment for £100,000 and consumed £25,000 of services in each of the first two quarters. Then they consumed a further £50,000 in the third quarter alone, and then $40,000 in the final quarter of the year. You'll also see something marked as the "Consumption Allowance" on the diagram:

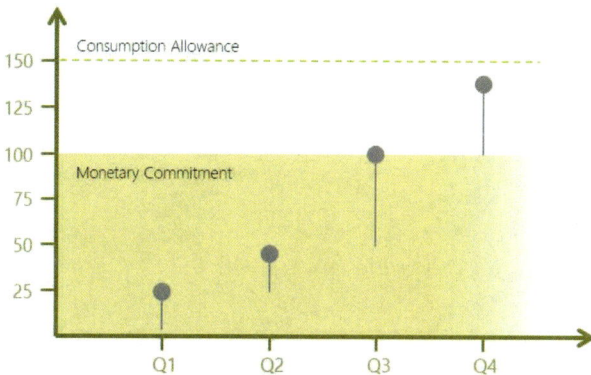

Figure 37: Azure Consumption Allowance

The Consumption Allowance is 50% of the original Monetary Commitment – so £50,000 in this case – and if the customer's overspend on Azure stays within the Consumption Allowance during the year then there are no penalties and the customer simply pays for the overspend at the end of the year at exactly the same rates as they paid through the year. So the Olive Oil Drum Company paid £100,000 at the start of the year and then at the end of the year would pay the remaining $40,000.

So the final example to consider is what happens when the overspend exceeds the Consumption Allowance. In the example below, Cerise Estate Management made a Monetary Commitment of £60,000 which meant that their Consumption Allowance was set at £90,000. They consumed £40,000 of services in each of the first two quarters keeping them within the Consumption Allowance at £80,000 but then exceeded it in quarters three and four with continued consumption at £40,000 per quarter.

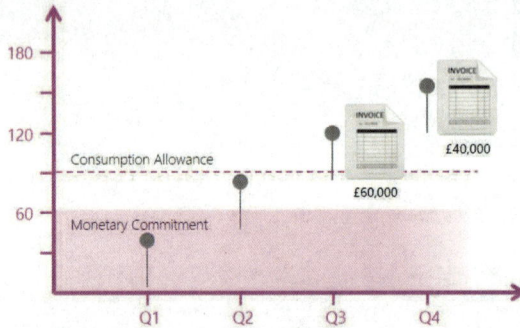

Figure 38: Azure Quarterly Billing

As soon as the Consumption Allowance is exceeded, the customer is switched to quarterly billing and at the end of the first quarter where the Consumption Allowance was exceeded they are invoiced for the full amount over the original Monetary Commitment. So, in the diagram above, there is an invoice issued at the end of Q3 for £60,000 – this is for the £120,000 that they have actually consumed minus the £60,000 they originally paid in the upfront Monetary Commitment. Another invoice is then issued at the end of the fourth quarter for the £40,000 of services they consumed in that quarter.

Note that in all of the examples above, the customer could choose to adjust their Monetary Commitment at anniversary for the following year – up or down – as required.

Also note that if Azure is purchased as an Additional Product in an EA the Monetary Commitment works in exactly the same way.

Applying your knowledge to the exam:

- Look out for business goals that specifically mention the products available through the SCE and see if the customer could commit to an SCE by being prepared to cover the whole of their installed base with SA for one, or more, products. There might be business objectives to run the latest version of the software, or a requirement for a particular SA benefit such as License Mobility, for example

- If you're asked to recommend the licenses that a customer would need on their initial order for an SCE remember that either L&SA or Subscription licenses can cover existing licenses without SA, and if Subscription licenses are used, the amounts may be reduced after 12 months

- If a customer has stated a desire to update their core infrastructure, remember that this term refers to Windows Server and System Center and is likely to be pointing you towards recommending that customers acquire the Core Infrastructure Server Suites through an SCE. Equally though, do remember that these suites ARE available through other agreements if a customer doesn't want to commit enterprise-wide

- You should learn the minimums as shown in the table at the beginning of this section so that you don't get caught out recommending an SCE when the minimums can't be reached

- Remember that the price level for an SCE is typically inherited from an existing agreement, so look out for details of a current Select Plus or Enterprise Agreement with a stated price level that would also apply to a new SCE

- Remember how the payments for Azure differ depending on how the customer buys it through the SCE: if they have an Azure-only SCE they then make an upfront Annual Monetary Commitment, if they have a non-Azure SCE then they pay quarterly in arrears

Recommending the Right Agreements

In the previous sections we considered the Volume Licensing agreements for large organizations separately; now let's compare the agreements side by side and see how you would apply this knowledge in the exam.

Many customers will have more than one Volume Licensing agreement dependent on what their business objectives are. For instance, if they have decided to deploy Office Professional Plus 2013 with SA throughout their organization but rarely buy SA on their server licenses, they are likely to have an Enterprise Agreement to cover their desktops, with an MPSA or Select Plus agreement running alongside for their ad hoc server license purchases. Equally, they could be a highly committed customer with an EA to cover their desktops, as well as a Server and Cloud Enrollment, or they may not see any benefit in SA at all, and sign an MPSA or Select Plus agreement for all of their license purchases.

Since we're considering all the LORG Volume Licensing agreements in this section I've grouped the following points into topics, rather than presenting you with a large and probably rather daunting single list! As usual, there are no new pieces of information covered, it's just a way to put the last few sections into context and help you to focus on the key points for the exam.

Applying your knowledge to the exam:

Perpetual v non-perpetual licenses:

- Look out for business goals that give you the aspirations of the company – are they happiest owning assets like licenses (recommend one of the perpetual agreements) or do they prefer to rent or lease (in which case recommend the Enterprise Subscription Agreement)

- Look out for the word "commitment" – an Enterprise Subscription Agreement represents a type of commitment since a customer needs to renew the agreement to continue to use the software, and so if the business goals state that a customer does not want any on-going commitment, you should recommend a perpetual agreement

- Look carefully in the future plans section of the customer scenarios and if there is an implication that the customer wants a one-off licensing agreement to acquire licenses to use for the foreseeable future then recommend a perpetual agreement

Standardization:

- Look out for business goals that tell you the organization's attitude to committing to a Microsoft desktop enterprise-wide and if this is important to them, then recommend an Enterprise Agreement. If you feel that the organization is happier purchasing licenses on a more transactional basis, then recommend an MPSA or Select Plus agreement

Software Assurance:

- Look out for business goals that state the organization's interest in, or preference for, Software Assurance. If they are interested, recommend an Enterprise Agreement and use other business goals to choose between the perpetual and subscription EA. If they want the flexibility to purchase licenses with or without Software Assurance, then recommend an MPSA or Select Plus agreement

- If an organization is particularly interested in Software Assurance, remember that customers get the most SA benefits when they buy their licenses through an Enterprise Agreement. The exception to this is when a customer has enrolled into MPSA or Select Plus SAM when the benefits are identical to an EA

Payment options:

- Look out for business goals where the organization has a particular requirement for a specific payment method – if they need spread payments then you can immediately disregard an MPSA or Select Plus agreement without SA as a recommended licensing solution for them

- Look out for business goals where the organization wants pro-rated annual pricing – this is another way of describing spread payments

- If you see a statement that relates to an organization wanting predictable costs then this is likely to lead to a recommendation for spread payments since the payments stay the same each year

- Additionally, watch out for an organization that wants to reduce their outgoings in the first year of deployment of new software as this too indicates a desire for spread payments. If it's stated specifically that the organization wants the lowest up-front costs then recommend an Enterprise Subscription Agreement

- Look out for statements that indicate the organization's attitude to buying their software. For example, if they don't mind making upfront payments, or want the flexibility to pay for software on a transactional basis so that they can purchase licenses as the business needs evolve, you would need to recommend an MPSA or Select Plus agreement

- Look out for business goals that express concern about the amount of expenditure when paying for license costs completely up front. A customer's anxiety about cash flow would also mean that spread payments may be of interest to them

Discounts:

- If you're asked to recommend an agreement purely on price, remember that an MPSA or Select Plus agreement will be the most expensive, followed by the perpetual EA, and then the Enterprise Subscription Agreement will be the most cost-effective

Multiple license acquisition methods:

- Although a Volume Licensing agreement is typically going to be the recommended way of acquiring licenses for the organizations that you'll come across in the exam, don't completely discount OEM licenses. If you see business goals that state a requirement to refresh hardware, then you should certainly consider recommending that Windows licenses are acquired in this way since this is going to be the most cost-effective solution. However, if a customer has existing Office licenses acquired through a Volume Licensing agreement then they could reassign those to their new machines and thus wouldn't need to buy OEM Office licenses

- Although the Enterprise Agreements are governed by Qualified Devices/Users and Enterprise Products, don't forget that Additional Products can still be purchased through these agreements. There would be no need for a customer to have a separate MPSA or Select Plus agreement for these licenses – unless of course they wanted to purchase licenses without SA, which would be a valid reason to have both agreements. The most common scenario you are likely to come across when recommending multiple agreements is when customers have an EA covering the desktop and then buy their server licenses through an MPSA or Select Plus agreement

ISV, SPLA and MOSA

Throughout this section we've focused on the Volume Licensing programs available for LORG customers. The exam focusses on these commercial agreements but you should also understand when customers may acquire licenses through three other programs.

The first is the Independent Software Vendor or ISV program. This program is aimed at software developers who need a way to integrate Microsoft products into their business applications and to distribute a fully-licensed solution to their customers. As an example, a development company may build a solution that relies on SQL Server, and the ISV program allows them to sell one license to their customer that licenses that customer for the bespoke solution as well as the underlying SQL Server license.

The second is the Service Provider License Agreement or SPLA program. This program allows hosting partners to license Microsoft products on a monthly basis to provide services and hosted applications to their customers. As an example, a customer could choose to deploy Exchange Server for email on their own premises in a traditional deployment, or they could decide that a hosted solution would suit their needs better and buy a subscription to Exchange hosted by a partner. The SPLA program is the way that the hosting partner pays Microsoft for the licenses that they are, in effect, renting to their customers.

And the third program to have some knowledge about is the Microsoft Online Subscription Agreement or MOSA. This agreement was shown on the Volume Licensing Agreements overview diagram on page 123 and for a few years it existed as the only way for customers to buy their Online Services licenses when they had one of the other Volume Licensing agreements. Nowadays, however, these other agreements (with the exception of Select Plus) allow organizations to purchase Online Services as well as licenses for on-premises products and as it's obviously more convenient to buy licenses through a single agreement, the MOSA is less-used.

Applying your knowledge to the exam:

- Many of the exam questions relating to these programs are straightforward and you'll simply be asked to recommend how a customer should acquire a license for a particular product based on third party solutions (ISV), or a hosted solution (SPLA)

- Remember that it is more convenient for customers to buy all of their licenses under one agreement and so a recommendation of MOSA is unlikely to be the best answer in a given scenario in the exam. You should always recommend one of the other agreements even if the customer has no existing Volume Licensing agreement as they will be able to buy on-premises licenses as well at a later date

- You may need to pick out why a particular program is NOT the best way for a customer to acquire a license. For example, a customer who wants perpetual licenses for products would not choose to license through SPLA, or if they needed SQL Server to support a range of line of business applications, then a license acquired through ISV tied to one custom application would not be sufficient

Agreements for Small and Medium Businesses

You will find some questions in the exam that ask you to recommend a Volume Licensing agreement for Small and Medium Businesses, or SMBs. In Microsoft terms this is typically an organization with less than 250 PCs and you should use this definition for the exam. As you know, the exam is primarily focused on recommending agreements to LORGs, so you don't need a detailed knowledge of the SMB programs, you'll just need to recommend an agreement for a smaller organization, based on some simple criteria. If you know and understand the LORG agreements, then consider that an Open agreement is the SMB version of an MPSA/Select Plus agreement, an Open Value Company Wide agreement the SMB version of an Enterprise Agreement, and the Open Value Subscription agreement the equivalent of the Enterprise Subscription Agreement. Applying what you know about the LORG programs will help you to choose the right SMB agreement in the exam.

You'll find a summary table of the SMB agreements in the Revision Cards section; note that this is a simplified table of information which just gives the level of detail you need for the exam, rather than being exhaustive. You'll see that one of the major differences in the SMB and LORG agreements is the way that affiliates are treated; in the SMB programs they must all be in the same geographic territory, but in the LORG programs they can be across the world.

Applying your knowledge in the exam:

- Pay attention to the size of the organization; don't assume that because it's an exam focused on recommending licensing solutions to LORGs that all scenarios will require a recommendation of a Select Plus or Enterprise Agreement. If the organization has under 250 PCs then you should be choosing an Open, Open Value, or Open Value Subscription agreement

The Microsoft Licensing Agreements Revision Cards

The following pages contain the Revision Cards for this section, providing a summary of the key points that you should know about the Volume Licensing agreements for the exam.

Revision Card 20:
Microsoft Volume Licensing Programs

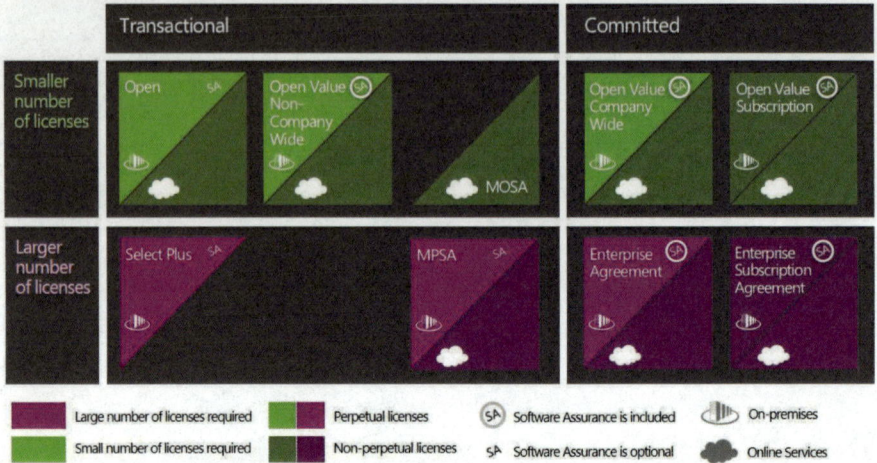

	Transactional			Committed	
Smaller number of licenses	Open Ⓢᴬ	Open Value Ⓢᴬ Non-Company Wide	MOSA	Open Value Ⓢᴬ Company Wide	Open Value Ⓢᴬ Subscription
Larger number of licenses	Select Plus Ⓢᴬ		MPSA Ⓢᴬ	Enterprise Agreement Ⓢᴬ	Enterprise Subscription Agreement Ⓢᴬ

Legend:
- Large number of licenses required
- Small number of licenses required
- Perpetual licenses
- Non-perpetual licenses
- Ⓢᴬ Software Assurance is included
- Sᴬ Software Assurance is optional
- On-premises
- Online Services

Revision Card 21:
Reasons to purchase licenses through Volume Licensing programs

Feature	Benefits of Volume Licensing
Availability	All products are available through the LORG Volume Licensing programs
Cost	License prices are generally more cost-effective and discounts are available for volume purchases
Downgrade Rights	Included with all licenses for on-premises software purchased through Volume Licensing programs
Upgrade Rights	Included with all licenses purchased with SA
License Reassignment Rights	Typically, licenses acquired through Volume Licensing programs may be reassigned every 90 days
Reimaging Rights	Only available to customers with a Volume Licensing agreement
License Manageability	The Volume Licensing portals help customers manage licenses acquired through Volume Licensing programs

Revision Card 22:
Select Plus, MPSA and Enterprise Agreements

	Select Plus and MPSA	Enterprise Agreement	Enterprise Subscription Agreement
Minimum Order	500 points or 250 USLs for MPSA	250 PCs or 250 USLs	250 PCs
Agreement Term	Evergreen	3 years	3 years
License Type	Perpetual	Perpetual	Non-perpetual
Agreement Type	Transactional	Committed	Committed
Software Assurance	Optional	Included	Included
Desktop Standardization	No	Required	Required
Price Bands	4 levels	4 levels	4 levels
Other Discounts	No	Platform	Platform
Payment Terms	Upfront or Spread Payments with SA	Spread Payments	Spread Payments
Affiliates	Across territories	Across territories	Across territories

Revision Card 23:
Select Plus and MPSA Price Levels

Points	Price Level
500	A
4,000	B
10,000	C
25,000	D

Revision Card 24:
Enterprise Agreements Price Levels

Qualified Devices/Users	Price Level
250	A
2,400	B
6,000	C
15,000	D

Revision Card 25:
Office 365 Add-ons in the Enterprise Agreement

	Core CAL Suite	Core CAL Suite + Office Professional Plus	Enterprise CAL Suite	Enterprise CAL Suite + Office Professional Plus
E1	✔	✔		
E3		✔		✔
E3 without O365 ProPlus	✔	✔	✔	✔
E4		✔		✔
E4 without O365 ProPlus	✔	✔	✔	✔

Revision Card 26:
Office 365 Transitions in the Enterprise Agreement

Existing Licenses	Transition
Core CAL Suite	E1 + Core CAL Bridge for Office 365
Core CAL Suite + Office Professional Plus 2013	E3 + Core CAL Bridge for Office 365
Enterprise CAL Suite + Office Professional Plus 2013	E3 + Enterprise CAL Bridge for Office 365

Revision Card 27:
The Server and Cloud Enrollment

Components	Application Platform	Core Infrastructure	Developer Tools	Azure
Products	SQL Server + optionally BizTalk and/or SharePoint	Windows Server and System Center	Visual Studio	Microsoft Azure Services
Minimums	**SQL:** 5 Servers and 250 CALs, or 50 Cores **SharePoint:** 5 Servers **BizTalk:** 24 Cores	25 Core Infrastructure Server Suites	20 licenses of Visual Studio Premium and/or Ultimate	$1,200 Annual Monetary Commitment
Commitment	SA on installed base	SA on installed base	SA on installed base	Upfront Monetary Commitment
Licenses Available	SA-only – for existing licenses with active SA L&SA – perpetual license option for existing licenses with no SA, or new licenses MSU – subscription license option for existing licenses with no SA, or new licenses Microsoft Azure Services – pay for consumption at the end of each quarter			Monetary Commitment SKU

Revision Card 28:
Other Licensing Programs

Program	Description
ISV	The Independent Software Vendor program is aimed at software developers who need a way to integrate Microsoft products into their business applications and to distribute a fully-licensed solution to their customers
SPLA	The Service Provider License Agreement allows hosting partners to license Microsoft products on a monthly basis to provide services and hosted applications to their customers
MOSA	The Microsoft Online Subscription Agreement is the agreement that a customer signs when they purchase, for example, Office 365 subscription licenses which cannot be acquired through a Select Plus agreement

Revision Card 29:
Open and Open Value Agreements

	Open	Open Value Company Wide	Open Value Subscription
Minimum Order	5 licenses	5 PCs	5 PCs
Agreement Term	2 years	3 years	3 years
License Type	Perpetual	Perpetual	Non-perpetual
Agreement Type	Transactional	Committed	Committed
Software Assurance	Optional	Included	Included
Desktop Standardization	No	Required	Required
Other Discounts	No	Platform	Platform
Payment Terms	Upfront	Spread Payments	Spread Payments
Affiliates	Same territory	Same territory	Same territory

Recap Questions and Answers

Use these Recap Questions to see how much you know about the Microsoft Volume Licensing agreements. If you find any areas that you need to go over you can review the relevant topic in this section of the book. Again, you'll find a couple of questions on each page with the answers when you turn over.

Questions 1 – 3

1. Purple Paint Pot Decorators have 800 PCs and they want to purchase Office 2013 licenses for all of them. They currently have a policy of owning all company assets and they are interested in a number of SA benefits. What licensing agreement is likely to be the best fit for them to purchase these licenses through?

   a) Select Plus
   b) Enterprise Agreement
   c) Enterprise Subscription Agreement
   d) MPSA

2. Blue Lamp Ideas are looking to purchase 540 licenses of Office 2013 for their head office machines. They have 1,000 machines in total and want to cover the 540 licenses with SA to make sure that they get new version rights. How would you recommend that they purchase these 540 licenses?

   a) Select Plus
   b) Enterprise Agreement
   c) Enterprise Subscription Agreement
   d) MPSA

3. Periwinkle Packaging Solutions are a small startup company with 15 brand new machines that have Windows 8.1 and Office 2013 pre-installed. They have set up a server infrastructure and now need to buy the Core CAL Suite for all of the machines. They have decided to invest in Software Assurance but need the very lowest upfront costs. How should they purchase these Core CAL Suite licenses?

   a) OEM
   b) Open with SA
   c) Open Value Company Wide
   d) Open Value Subscription

Answers 1 – 3

1. Purple Paint Pot Decorators have 800 PCs and they want to purchase Office 2013 licenses for all of them. They currently have a policy of owning all company assets and they are interested in a number of SA benefits. What licensing agreement is likely to be the best fit for them to purchase these licenses through?

   a) Select Plus
   b) **Enterprise Agreement** ✓
   c) Enterprise Subscription Agreement
   d) MPSA

2. Blue Lamp Ideas are looking to purchase 540 licenses of Office 2013 for their head office machines. They have 1,000 machines in total and want to cover the 540 licenses with SA to make sure that they get new version rights. How would you recommend that they purchase these 540 licenses?

   a) Select Plus
   b) Enterprise Agreement
   c) Enterprise Subscription Agreement
   d) **MPSA** ✓

3. Periwinkle Packaging Solutions are a small startup company with 15 brand new machines that have Windows 8.1 and Office 2013 pre-installed. They have set up a server infrastructure and now need to buy the Core CAL Suite for all of the machines. They have decided to invest in Software Assurance but need the very lowest upfront costs. How should they purchase these Core CAL Suite licenses?

   a) OEM
   b) Open with SA
   c) Open Value Company Wide
   d) **Open Value Subscription** ✓

Questions 4 – 6

4. Ultramarine Swim Wear have purchased 300 PCs with Windows 8.1 pre-installed and now want to buy Office 2013 licenses for these machines. They want to pay an annual fee for these licenses and, if the number of PCs goes down, they would like to pay a smaller annual fee. What licensing agreement is likely to be the best fit for them to purchase these licenses through?

    a) Select Plus
    b) Enterprise Agreement
    c) Enterprise Subscription Agreement
    d) Open Value Subscription

5. Maroon Balloons have signed a Server and Cloud Enrollment for the Core Infrastructure component. They have been automatically provisioned for Azure and start using the services. When are they charged for their consumption?

    a) They must make a Monetary Commitment at the time they start using the service
    b) Invoices are issued monthly
    c) Invoices are issued quarterly
    d) They true up their usage at the end of the year

6. Cyan Ida's Pharmacy have decided to purchase their software licenses through a Volume Licensing program. Which of the following are benefits of purchasing through a Volume Licensing program? Choose two answers.

    a) Downgrade rights
    b) Rights to use software for ever
    c) Reimaging rights
    d) Unlimited end user support

Answers 4 – 6

4. Ultramarine Swim Wear have purchased 300 PCs with Windows 8.1 pre-installed and now want to buy Office 2013 licenses for these machines. They want to pay an annual fee for these licenses and, if the number of PCs goes down, they would like to pay a smaller annual fee. What licensing agreement is likely to be the best fit for them to purchase these licenses through?

   a) Select
   b) Enterprise Agreement
   c) **Enterprise Subscription Agreement** ✓
   d) Open Value Subscription

5. Maroon Balloons have signed a Server and Cloud Enrollment for the Core Infrastructure component. They have been automatically provisioned for Azure and start using the services. When are they charged for their consumption?

   a) They must make a Monetary Commitment at the time they start using the service
   b) Invoices are issued monthly
   c) **Invoices are issued quarterly** ✓
   d) They true up their usage at the end of the year

6. Cyan Ida's Pharmacy have decided to purchase their software licenses through a Volume Licensing program. Which of the following are benefits of purchasing through a Volume Licensing program? Choose two answers.

   a) **Downgrade rights** ✓
   b) Rights to use software for ever
   c) **Reimaging rights** ✓
   d) Unlimited end user support

Questions 7 – 9

7. Pink Champagne Limousines currently have 450 PCs which are licensed with Windows 8.1 Pro and Office Professional Plus 2013 bought through their MPSA. They intend to purchase 35 new machines which also need to be licensed for Windows and Office. How would you recommend that they purchase these new licenses?
    a) Both Windows and Office through OEM
    b) Windows through OEM and Office through the MPSA
    c) Both Windows and Office through the MPSA
    d) Windows through the MPSA and Office through OEM

8. Spring Green Grocers want to sign an MPSA and will be setting up various Purchasing Accounts to reflect the way that they want to purchase licenses as an organization. Which of the following may they set up as Purchasing Accounts? Choose three answers.
    a) The Purchasing division within Spring Green Grocers
    b) A supplier
    c) A wholly owned subsidiary
    d) A partner company of which they own 75%
    e) An associate organization of which they own 25%

9. Lightshades of Grey want to purchase some Office Professional Plus 2013 licenses with SA, some Windows Server 2012 R2 licenses without SA, and 50 CRM Online Basic USLs. What licensing program(s) would you recommend that they purchase these licenses through?
    a) MPSA
    b) Enterprise Agreement and MPSA
    c) Select Plus and MOSA
    d) Enterprise Agreement and MOSA

7. Pink Champagne Limousines currently have 450 PCs which are licensed with Windows 8.1 Pro and Office Professional Plus 2013 bought through their MPSA. They intend to purchase 35 new machines which also need to be licensed for Windows and Office. How would you recommend that they purchase these new licenses?

    a) Both Windows and Office through OEM
    b) **Windows through OEM and Office through the MPSA** ✓
    c) Both Windows and Office through the MPSA
    d) Windows through the MPSA and Office through OEM

8. Spring Green Grocers want to sign an MPSA and will be setting up various Purchasing Accounts to reflect the way that they want to purchase licenses as an organization. Which of the following may they set up as Purchasing Accounts? Choose three answers.

    a) **The Purchasing division within Spring Green Grocers** ✓
    b) A supplier
    c) **A wholly owned subsidiary** ✓
    d) **A partner company of which they own 75%** ✓
    e) An associate organization of which they own 25%

9. Lightshades of Grey want to purchase some Office Professional Plus 2013 licenses with SA, some Windows Server 2012 R2 licenses without SA, and 50 CRM Online Basic USLs. What licensing program(s) would you recommend that they purchase these licenses through?

    a) **MPSA** ✓
    b) Enterprise Agreement and MPSA
    c) Select Plus and MOSA
    d) Enterprise Agreement and MOSA

Questions 10 – 12

10. Fuchsia Fancy Dress Hire have an active Select Plus agreement through which they have purchased Office Professional Plus 2013 licenses for 500 PCs. 50 of these PCs are now being retired and will be replaced with new laptops. How would you recommend that they license Office Professional Plus 2013 for these new laptops?

   a) Reassign the existing licenses from the PCs that will be retired
   b) Buy Office Professional 2013 pre-installed on the new laptops
   c) Add SA to the existing licenses so that they can be reassigned to the new devices
   d) Buy an additional 50 Office Professional Plus 2013 licenses through their Select Plus agreement

11. Peach Snaps Cameras have a server farm consisting of 40 servers which they want to license with Windows Server and System Center covered with Software Assurance. How would you recommend that Peach Snaps Cameras acquire their licenses?

   a) Through an MPSA with Software Assurance Membership
   b) Through an Enterprise Subscription Agreement
   c) Through an Enrollment for Core Infrastructure
   d) Through a Server and Cloud Enrollment

12. Powderblue Pottery currently have 2,000 Qualified Devices and purchase their licenses through an Enterprise Agreement. They have ambitious growth plans and aim to open five sub-offices in the next year with 150 new PCs in each office. At the end of the year they are due to renew their Enterprise Agreement; what price level will they be entitled to if their ambitious growth plans are met?

   a) Level A
   b) Level B
   c) Level C
   d) Level D

Answers 10 – 12

10. Fuchsia Fancy Dress Hire have an active Select Plus agreement through which they have purchased Office Professional Plus 2013 licenses for 500 PCs. 50 of these PCs are now being retired and will be replaced with new laptops. How would you recommend that they license Office Professional Plus 2013 for these new laptops?
    a) **Reassign the existing licenses from the PCs that will be retired** ✓
    b) Buy Office Professional 2013 pre-installed on the new laptops
    c) Add SA to the existing licenses so that they can be reassigned to the new devices
    d) Buy an additional 50 Office Professional Plus 2013 licenses through their Select Plus agreement

11. Peach Snaps Cameras have a server farm consisting of 40 servers which they want to license with Windows Server and System Center covered with Software Assurance. How would you recommend that Peach Snaps Cameras acquire their licenses?
    a) Through an MPSA with Software Assurance Membership
    b) Through an Enterprise Subscription Agreement
    c) Through an Enrollment for Core Infrastructure
    d) **Through a Server and Cloud Enrollment** ✓

12. Powderblue Pottery currently have 2,000 Qualified Devices and purchase their licenses through an Enterprise Agreement. They have ambitious growth plans and aim to open five sub-offices in the next year with 150 new PCs in each office. At the end of the year they are due to renew their Enterprise Agreement; what price level will they be entitled to if their ambitious growth plans are met?
    a) Level A
    b) **Level B** ✓
    c) Level C
    d) Level D

Questions 13 – 15

13. Tangerine Truckers have signed a Server and Cloud Enrollment for SQL Server and opted to cover 15 servers with SQL Server 2014 Core Subscription licenses at the start of the agreement. When can they reduce the number of these Subscription licenses?

    a) At the first Anniversary
    b) At the second Anniversary
    c) At any time in the first year
    d) At renewal

14. World of Magnolia have 500 PCs which they want to license with non-perpetual licenses for Windows, Office and the Core CAL Suite. Which licensing program would you recommend that they purchase these licenses through?

    a) A Component MPSA
    b) A Component Enterprise Subscription Agreement
    c) A Platform Enterprise Subscription Agreement
    d) A Platform Enterprise Agreement

15. Copper Feel Fabrics have decided to purchase licenses through a Select Plus agreement and want to receive the maximum number of SA benefits. What should they do?

    a) Buy Software Assurance Plus
    b) Enroll into Software Assurance Membership
    c) They already receive the maximum number of SA benefits by buying licenses with SA through their Select Plus agreement
    d) Sign an additional SA Plus agreement

Answers 13 – 15

13. Tangerine Truckers have signed a Server and Cloud Enrollment for SQL Server and opted to cover 15 servers with SQL Server 2014 Core Subscription licenses at the start of the agreement. When can they reduce the number of these Subscription licenses?

    a) **At the first Anniversary** ✓
    b) At the second Anniversary
    c) At any time in the first year
    d) At renewal

14. World of Magnolia have 500 PCs which they want to license with non-perpetual licenses for Windows, Office and the Core CAL Suite. Which licensing program would you recommend that they purchase these licenses through?

    a) A Component MPSA
    b) A Component Enterprise Subscription Agreement
    c) **A Platform Enterprise Subscription Agreement** ✓
    d) A Platform Enterprise Agreement

15. Copper Feel Fabrics have decided to purchase licenses through a Select Plus agreement and want to receive the maximum number of SA benefits. What should they do?

    a) Buy Software Assurance Plus
    b) **Enroll into Software Assurance Membership** ✓
    c) They already receive the maximum number of SA benefits by buying licenses with SA through their Select Plus agreement
    d) Sign an additional SA Plus agreement

Questions 16 – 19

16. The Papaya Hire Company are deciding on the structure of their Purchasing Accounts as they set up their MPSA. How many partners may they assign to each Purchasing Account?

   a) 1
   b) 2
   c) 4
   d) As many as required

17. The Cobalt Bolt Company are interested in signing an Enterprise Agreement. How many PCs must they have to sign this agreement?

   a) 100
   b) 250
   c) 500
   d) 1,000

18. Honeydew Hatters completely own three companies, all located within five miles of their head office, with a total of 1,035 PCs. They want to implement a centralized purchasing policy under a single agreement so that all organizations are licensed in exactly the same way. What agreement should they sign to achieve this?

   a) An MPSA
   b) An Open Value agreement
   c) An Enterprise Agreement
   d) A Select Plus Affiliates Agreement

19. The Lemon Launderette are interested in signing an MPSA. How many USLs must they purchase in the first year to qualify for Level A pricing?

   a) 100
   b) 250
   c) 500
   d) The Price Level is set by the number of points not USLs

16. The Papaya Hire Company are deciding on the structure of their Purchasing Accounts as they set up their MPSA. How many partners may they assign to each Purchasing Account?

    a) 1
    b) 2
    c) 4
    d) **As many as required** ✓

17. The Cobalt Bolt Company are interested in signing an Enterprise Agreement. How many PCs must they have to sign this agreement?

    a) 100
    b) **250** ✓
    c) 500
    d) 1,000

18. Honeydew Hatters completely own three companies, all located within five miles of their head office, with a total of 1,035 PCs. They want to implement a centralized purchasing policy under a single agreement so that all organizations are licensed in exactly the same way. What agreement should they sign to achieve this?

    a) An MPSA
    b) An Open Value agreement
    c) **An Enterprise Agreement** ✓
    d) A Select Plus Affiliates Agreement

19. The Lemon Launderette are interested in signing an MPSA. How many USLs must they purchase in the first year to qualify for Level A pricing?

    a) 100
    b) **250** ✓
    c) 500
    d) The Price Level is set by the number of points not USLs

Questions 20 – 23

20. Vermilion Jewellers need some new Office licenses and have decided that they want perpetual licenses. Which of the following would allow them to purchase perpetual licenses? Choose two answers.

a) An MPSA
b) An Enterprise Subscription Agreement
c) Office 365
d) OEM

21. The Yellow Soup Tureen have an Enterprise Agreement. For how long can they purchase licenses under this agreement?

a) 1 year
b) 2 years
c) 3 years
d) The agreement is evergreen so they can purchase licenses for as long as they like

22. Xanthic Tractors are about to sign an Enterprise Agreement and are counting up their Qualified Devices. Which of the following devices do not need to be included? Choose two answers.

a) PCs that are only used to run their Hire Services software
b) PCs that are more than five years old
c) PCs that are not being used currently
d) PCs that are being used as a server

23. Which of the following are benefits of the MPSA? Choose two answers.

a) A consolidated view across all licensing assets
b) A single agreement to purchase both perpetual and non-perpetual licenses for on-premises software
c) A single agreement to purchase both licenses for on-premises software and Online Services
d) Discounts for committing to products deployed enterprise-wide

20. Vermilion Jewellers need some new Office licenses and have decided that they want perpetual licenses. Which of the following would allow them to purchase perpetual licenses? Choose two answers.

    a) **An MPSA** ✓
    b) An Enterprise Subscription Agreement
    c) Office 365
    d) **OEM** ✓

21. The Yellow Soup Tureen have an Enterprise Agreement. For how long can they purchase licenses under this agreement?

    a) 1 year
    b) 2 years
    c) **3 years** ✓
    d) The agreement is evergreen so they can purchase licenses for as long as they like

22. Xanthic Tractors are about to sign an Enterprise Agreement and are counting up their Qualified Devices. Which of the following devices do not need to be included? Choose two answers.

    a) **PCs that are only used to run their Hire Services software** ✓
    b) PCs that are more than five years old
    c) PCs that are not being used currently
    d) **PCs that are being used as a server** ✓

23. Which of the following are benefits of the MPSA? Choose two answers.

    a) **A consolidated view across all licensing assets** ✓
    b) A single agreement to purchase both perpetual and non-perpetual licenses for on-premises software
    c) **A single agreement to purchase both licenses for on-premises software and Online Services** ✓
    d) Discounts for committing to products deployed enterprise-wide

Questions 24 – 26

24. Mauve Stoves have an existing Enterprise Agreement for their 8,000 desktops and have always purchased their server licenses through a Select Plus agreement for which they have achieved Level B pricing. They now intend to sign a new Server and Cloud Enrollment since they want to upgrade their whole SQL Server estate of 50 servers to the latest version. What price level will they be entitled to for the new SCE?
    a) Level A
    b) Level B
    c) Level C
    d) Level D

25. Lilac Landscaping Services are an international garden design firm. They are about to sign a Platform EA for their desktops and have counted the following devices: 1,800 desktop PCs, 350 laptops and 350 Point of Sale terminals. What price level will they be entitled to in their new EA?
    a) Level A
    b) Level B
    c) Level C
    d) Level D

26. Taupe Telecoms feel that an Enterprise Agreement will best suit their licensing needs for the next three years, and they understand that they need to license at least one of the Enterprise Products for each of their Qualified Devices. Which of the following products are valid Enterprise Products? Choose three answers.
    a) Windows 8.1 Enterprise
    b) Windows Server 2012 R2
    c) Office Professional Plus 2013
    d) Core CAL Suite
    e) Windows Server 2012 CAL
    f) SQL Server 2014 CAL

24. Mauve Stoves have an existing Enterprise Agreement for their 8,000 desktops and have always purchased their server licenses through a Select Plus agreement for which they have achieved Level B pricing. They now intend to sign a new Server and Cloud Enrollment since they want to upgrade their whole SQL Server estate of 50 servers to the latest version. What price level will they be entitled to for the new SCE?
    a) Level A
    b) Level B
    c) **Level C ✓**
    d) Level D

25. Lilac Landscaping Services are an international garden design firm. They are about to sign a Platform EA for their desktops and have counted the following devices: 1,800 desktop PCs, 350 laptops and 350 Point of Sale terminals. What price level will they be entitled to in their new EA?
    a) **Level A ✓**
    b) Level B
    c) Level C
    d) Level D

26. Taupe Telecoms feel that an Enterprise Agreement will best suit their licensing needs for the next three years, and they understand that they need to license at least one of the Enterprise Products for each of their Qualified Devices. Which of the following products are valid Enterprise Products? Choose three answers.
    a) **Windows 8.1 Enterprise ✓**
    b) Windows Server 2012 R2
    c) **Office Professional Plus 2013 ✓**
    d) **Core CAL Suite ✓**
    e) Windows Server 2012 CAL
    f) SQL Server 2014 CAL

Questions 27 – 29

27. Goldfinger Food have signed an Azure-only Server and Cloud Enrollment and have made a Monetary Commitment of £50,000. During the third quarter they exceed their Monetary Commitment by £10,000. When do they pay for this overspend?

    a) At the point in time that they exceed the Monetary Commitment
    b) At the end of the quarter in which the overspend occurred
    c) At the end of the year
    d) There is no facility for them to overspend; they must make an additional Monetary Commitment when funds run out

28. Sienna Blenders have approximately 150 PCs. They want to standardize on Office Professional Plus 2013 on all PCs with perpetual licenses with Software Assurance. What licensing program are they likely to find a good fit to purchase licenses through?

    a) MPSA
    b) Open Value Company-Wide
    c) Enterprise Agreement
    d) Standard Office Agreement

29. Apple and Pears Stairlifts want to acquire Exchange Server licenses and 567 CALs for their on-premises email server. How would you recommend that they acquire the licenses for this deployment?

    a) Through an MPSA
    b) Through a SPLA agreement
    c) Through an ISV agreement
    d) Through MOSA

27. Goldfinger Food have signed an Azure-only Server and Cloud Enrollment and have made a Monetary Commitment of £50,000. During the third quarter they exceed their Monetary Commitment by £10,000. When do they pay for this overspend?

    a) At the point in time that they exceed the Monetary Commitment
    b) At the end of the quarter in which the overspend occurred
    c) **At the end of the year** ✓
    d) There is no facility for them to overspend; they must make an additional Monetary Commitment when funds run out

28. Sienna Blenders have approximately 150 PCs. They want to standardize on Office Professional Plus 2013 on all PCs with perpetual licenses with Software Assurance. What licensing program are they likely to find a good fit to purchase licenses through?

    a) MPSA
    b) **Open Value Company-Wide** ✓
    c) Enterprise Agreement
    d) Standard Office Agreement

29. Apple and Pears Stairlifts want to acquire Exchange Server licenses and 567 CALs for their on-premises email server. How would you recommend that they acquire the licenses for this deployment?

    a) **Through an MPSA** ✓
    b) Through a SPLA agreement
    c) Through an ISV agreement
    d) Through MOSA

Questions 30 – 32

30. The Mala Kite Shop own 411 devices that employees use either in the head office or at home. They want to upgrade the version of Office on 245 of these devices and want to pay for the licenses in full at this point so that they know that they don't owe any money or have any commitment to pay anything later. They are not looking to upgrade the version for another four or five years. Through which agreement would you recommend that they purchase these licenses?

   a) Select Plus
   b) MPSA
   c) Enterprise Agreement
   d) Enterprise Subscription Agreement

31. How is the Consumption Allowance calculated for a customer who has made a Monetary Commitment to Azure?

   a) It is £10,000 or 10% of the Monetary Commitment, whichever is greater
   b) It is 25% of the Monetary Commitment
   c) It is 50% of the Monetary Commitment
   d) It is based on the Price Level of the SCE

32. Coff E-Learning Solutions have ten SharePoint Servers and CALs for 500 users. They want to sign an SCE but have been told that they can't. Why is this?

   a) They do not have enough SharePoint Servers to meet the minimum requirements for the SCE
   b) They can't sign an SCE for SharePoint Server without including SQL Server
   c) SharePoint Server is not available to be purchased under the SCE
   d) They do not have active Software Assurance on their SharePoint Servers

30. The Mala Kite Shop own 411 devices that employees use either in the head office or at home. They want to upgrade the version of Office on 245 of these devices and want to pay for the licenses in full at this point so that they know that they don't owe any money or have any commitment to pay anything later. They are not looking to upgrade the version for another four or five years. Through which agreement would you recommend that they purchase these licenses?

    a) Select Plus
    b) **MPSA** ✓
    c) Enterprise Agreement
    d) Enterprise Subscription Agreement

31. How is the Consumption Allowance calculated for a customer who has made a Monetary Commitment to Azure?

    a) It is £10,000 or 10% of the Monetary Commitment, whichever is greater
    b) It is 25% of the Monetary Commitment
    c) **It is 50% of the Monetary Commitment** ✓
    d) It is based on the Price Level of the SCE

32. Coff E-Learning Solutions have ten SharePoint Servers and CALs for 500 users. They want to sign an SCE but have been told that they can't. Why is this?

    a) They do not have enough SharePoint Servers to meet the minimum requirements for the SCE
    b) **They can't sign an SCE for SharePoint Server without including SQL Server** ✓
    c) SharePoint Server is not available to be purchased under the SCE
    d) They do not have active Software Assurance on their SharePoint Servers

Questions 33 – 35

33. The Olive Oil Drum Company have a Windows-based server farm and want to sign a Server and Cloud Enrollment for the Core Infrastructure component. What licenses will they need if they have ten four-processor servers all licensed with Windows Standard with no active SA?
    a) 40 CIS Standard without Windows Server L&SA
    b) 20 CIS Standard L&SA
    c) 40 CIS Standard L&SA
    d) 20 CIS Standard SA

34. The Raspberry Rubicon are preparing to refresh their software estate and have identified the following requirements: Office Professional Plus 2013 with SA, and Core CAL licenses for all of their 1,250 PCs; 10 Windows Server 2012 R2 licenses; 4 Exchange Server 2013 licenses; and 2 SharePoint 2013 licenses. How would you recommend that they acquire these licenses?
    a) Sign an Enterprise Agreement for all of the licenses
    b) Sign an Enterprise Agreement for the PCs and an MPSA for the server licenses
    c) Sign an MPSA for all of the licenses
    d) Sign an Enterprise Agreement for the server licenses and an MPSA for the PCs

35. Mellow Yellow Sounds have an existing Enterprise Agreement for the Core CAL Suite licensed per user. They now want to add Online Services for some of their users. Which of the following Add-ons may they purchase? Choose three answers.
    a) E1
    b) E3
    c) E3 without Office 365 ProPlus
    d) E4
    e) E4 without Office 365 ProPlus

33. The Olive Oil Drum Company have a Windows-based server farm and want to sign a Server and Cloud Enrollment for the Core Infrastructure component. What licenses will they need if they have ten four-processor servers all licensed with Windows Standard with no active SA?

    a) 40 CIS Standard without Windows Server L&SA
    b) **20 CIS Standard L&SA** ✓
    c) 40 CIS Standard L&SA
    d) 20 CIS Standard SA

34. The Raspberry Rubicon are preparing to refresh their software estate and have identified the following requirements: Office Professional Plus 2013 with SA, and Core CAL licenses for all of their 1,250 PCs; 10 Windows Server 2012 R2 licenses; 4 Exchange Server 2013 licenses; and 2 SharePoint 2013 licenses. How would you recommend that they acquire these licenses?

    a) Sign an Enterprise Agreement for all of the licenses
    b) **Sign an Enterprise Agreement for the PCs and an MPSA for the server licenses** ✓
    c) Sign an MPSA for all of the licenses
    d) Sign an Enterprise Agreement for the server licenses and an MPSA for the PCs

35. Mellow Yellow Sounds have an existing Enterprise Agreement for the Core CAL Suite licensed per user. They now want to add Online Services for some of their users. Which of the following Add-ons may they purchase? Choose three answers.

    a) **E1** ✓
    b) E3
    c) **E3 without Office 365 ProPlus** ✓
    d) E4
    e) **E4 without Office 365 ProPlus** ✓

36. Amaranth Antiques want to upgrade their server estate to the latest versions of the software and are considering a Server and Cloud Enrollment. They are interested in enrolling SharePoint Server, SQL Server, BizTalk Server, CRM Server, and Exchange Server in the agreement. Which products may be included? Choose three answers.

   a) SharePoint Server
   b) SQL Server
   c) BizTalk Server
   d) CRM Server
   e) Exchange Server

37. The Jazzberry Jam Shop have an Enterprise Subscription Agreement that is coming to the end of its term. They understand that one of the options that they have at the end of their ESA is to convert the subscription licenses into perpetual licenses. What is the term for this process?

   a) Buy-out
   b) Buy-in
   c) True Up
   d) True Out

38. Myrtle Beachwear have decided on the licenses that they need to complete their latest server deployment project and want to acquire the licenses through an MPSA since they will not be committing to SA on every license. Their points total for their initial order is 2,750. What price level will this entitle them to?

   a) Level A
   b) Level B
   c) Level C
   d) Level D

36. Amaranth Antiques want to upgrade their server estate to the latest versions of the software and are considering a Server and Cloud Enrollment. They are interested in enrolling SharePoint Server, SQL Server, BizTalk Server, CRM Server, and Exchange Server in the agreement. Which products may be included? Choose three answers.

    a) **SharePoint Server** ✓
    b) **SQL Server** ✓
    c) **BizTalk Server** ✓
    d) CRM Server
    e) Exchange Server

37. The Jazzberry Jam Shop have an Enterprise Subscription Agreement that is coming to the end of its term. They understand that one of the options that they have at the end of their ESA is to convert the subscription licenses into perpetual licenses. What is the term for this process?

    a) **Buy-out** ✓
    b) Buy-in
    c) True Up
    d) True Out

38. Myrtle Beachwear have decided on the licenses that they need to complete their latest server deployment project and want to acquire the licenses through an MPSA since they will not be committing to SA on every license. Their points total for their initial order is 2,750. What price level will this entitle them to?

    a) **Level A** ✓
    b) Level B
    c) Level C
    d) Level D

Questions 39 – 41

39. Charcoal Chimney Sweeps are considering what they need from a Volume Licensing agreement. Which of the following would lead you to specifically recommend a Select Plus agreement? Choose three answers.

a) They want to buy perpetual licenses for on-premises software
b) They want to buy licenses on an ad hoc basis
c) They want to buy subscription licenses for Online Services
d) They want to buy SA on all licenses
e) They want to allow affiliates to purchase under the same agreement

40. Ochre Poker want to upgrade their existing SQL Server licenses to the latest version. Unfortunately they don't have Software Assurance on these licenses. Which Volume Licensing program will minimize the upgrade costs for them?

a) Enterprise Agreement
b) Enrollment for Application Platform
c) Server and Cloud Enrollment
d) Enterprise Subscription Agreement

41. The Bondi Blue Bistro have purchased Windows Server 2012 R2 licenses with Software Assurance through their MPSA. What payment options are available to them? Choose two answers.

a) Payment upfront
b) Spread monthly payments
c) Payment at the end of the agreement term
d) Spread annual payments

39. Charcoal Chimney Sweeps are considering what they need from a Volume Licensing agreement. Which of the following would lead you to specifically recommend a Select Plus agreement? Choose three answers.

    a) **They want to buy perpetual licenses for on-premises software** ✓
    b) **They want to buy licenses on an ad hoc basis** ✓
    c) They want to buy subscription licenses for Online Services
    d) They want to buy SA on all licenses
    e) **They want to allow affiliates to purchase under the same agreement** ✓

40. Ochre Poker want to upgrade their existing SQL Server licenses to the latest version. Unfortunately they don't have Software Assurance on these licenses. Which Volume Licensing program will minimize the upgrade costs for them?

    a) Enterprise Agreement
    b) Enrollment for Application Platform
    c) **Server and Cloud Enrollment** ✓
    d) Enterprise Subscription Agreement

41. The Bondi Blue Bistro have purchased Windows Server 2012 R2 licenses with Software Assurance through their MPSA. What payment options are available to them? Choose two answers.

    a) **Payment upfront** ✓
    b) Spread monthly payments
    c) Payment at the end of the agreement term
    d) **Spread annual payments** ✓

Questions 42 – 44

42. Blacken White Solicitors have an Enterprise Agreement with the Enterprise CAL Suite and Office Professional Plus 2013 that they want to transition to Office 365. What licenses will they have after the transition has taken place? Choose two answers.
    a) Enterprise CAL Suite
    b) Office 365 Plan E3
    c) Enterprise CAL Suite Bridge for Office 365
    d) Office 365 Plan E4

43. Pastel Pink Personal Coaches want to buy 125 Office 365 E1 licenses and 140 Office 365 E3 licenses. For which of the following agreements is this a valid initial order? Choose two answers.
    a) MPSA
    b) Select Plus
    c) Enterprise Agreement
    d) Server and Cloud Enrollment

44. Turquoise Toys want to sign a Server and Cloud Enrollment with the SQL Server component. Which of the following represent the correct minimum requirements for SQL Server? Choose two answers.
    a) 5 Servers and 250 CALs
    b) 40 Core licenses
    c) 50 Core licenses
    d) 5 Servers and 500 CALs
    e) 50 Core licenses and 5 Servers

42. Blacken White Solicitors have an Enterprise Agreement with the Enterprise CAL Suite and Office Professional Plus 2013 that they want to transition to Office 365. What licenses will they have after the transition has taken place? Choose two answers.
    a) Enterprise CAL Suite
    b) **Office 365 Plan E3** ✓
    c) **Enterprise CAL Suite Bridge for Office 365** ✓
    d) Office 365 Plan E4

43. Pastel Pink Personal Coaches want to buy 125 Office 365 E1 licenses and 140 Office 365 E3 licenses. For which of the following agreements is this a valid initial order? Choose two answers.
    a) **MPSA** ✓
    b) Select Plus
    c) **Enterprise Agreement** ✓
    d) Server and Cloud Enrollment

44. Turquoise Toys want to sign a Server and Cloud Enrollment with the SQL Server component. Which of the following represent the correct minimum requirements for SQL Server? Choose two answers.
    a) **5 Servers and 250 CALs** ✓
    b) 40 Core licenses
    c) **50 Core licenses** ✓
    d) 5 Servers and 500 CALs
    e) 50 Core licenses and 5 Servers

Questions 45 – 46

45. Aisle of White Paints are interested in acquiring their licenses through a program that offers discounted pricing for standardizing on a Microsoft platform product. Which of the following programs offer this? Choose two answers.

   a) Open
   b) Enterprise Agreement
   c) MPSA
   d) Enterprise Subscription Agreement

46. Fandango Fitness have a SQL Server Standard estate licensed with the Server / CAL model. They currently have ten servers but are expecting to retire three in the short to medium term. They have SA on two of the servers that they will not retire and prefer to own licensing assets where it makes commercial sense. What would be the best option for their initial order on an SCE?

   a) 2 SQL Server SA, 3 SQL Server MSU, 5 SQL Server L&SA
   b) 10 SQL Server L&SA
   c) 2 SQL Server SA, 8 SQL Server L&SA
   d) 2 SQL Server SA, 8 SQL Server MSU

45. Aisle of White Paints are interested in acquiring their licenses through a program that offers discounted pricing for standardizing on a Microsoft platform product. Which of the following programs offer this? Choose two answers.

    a) Open
    b) **Enterprise Agreement** ✓
    c) MPSA
    d) **Enterprise Subscription Agreement** ✓

46. Fandango Fitness have a SQL Server Standard estate licensed with the Server / CAL model. They currently have ten servers but are expecting to retire three in the short to medium term. They have SA on two of the servers that they will not retire and prefer to own licensing assets where it makes commercial sense. What would be the best option for their initial order on an SCE?

    a) **2 SQL Server SA, 3 SQL Server MSU, 5 SQL Server L&SA** ✓
    b) 10 SQL Server L&SA
    c) 2 SQL Server SA, 8 SQL Server L&SA
    d) 2 SQL Server SA, 8 SQL Server MSU

PART 4: SOFTWARE ASSURANCE

For the exam (and real life!) you need to be confident with all of the SA benefits in terms of what they offer an organization and the business goals that they would meet. You may already know that the benefits available to customers differ dependent on the Volume Licensing agreement that they purchase their licenses through, but this is not really a focus for the exam since the benefits are largely the same through the Select Plus, MPSA and Enterprise Agreements, and exactly the same if a Select Plus or MPSA customer commits to Software Assurance Membership – buying SA on all licenses in a particular pool. You should instead be ready to pick out the most appropriate benefit to match it to the needs of the business as a whole or an individual department.

If you find you want more information outside of that required for the exam, you should refer to the Microsoft Product List or the MPSA Licensing Manual which has lots of information about all of the SA benefits.

If you are already familiar with the SA benefits, why not skip to the Recap Questions on page 248 and test yourself?

Buying Software Assurance

Software Assurance can only be purchased through Volume Licensing agreements; it's an optional purchase in Select Plus and MPSA agreements, and compulsory in the Enterprise Agreements as we saw in Part 3 of this book. Customers who purchase licenses with Software Assurance during an agreement may choose to renew just the SA at the end of the agreement, and if they continue to renew the SA, then they will never need to purchase another license for that product again.

It's worth noting that if you buy licenses through a Volume Licensing agreement you must decide at the point of purchase if you want to include SA or not; there is no option to add on SA at a later date. This is different to purchasing licenses through the OEM channel where a customer typically (and always for the purposes of the exam) has 90 days to add SA to a license – often known as a grace period. If they don't have a Volume Licensing agreement they would need to start an MPSA or Select Plus agreement and all the usual program rules would apply.

Software Assurance benefits are allocated automatically to organizations as they buy licenses through their Volume Licensing agreements. Customers then manage these benefits through one of the Volume Licensing portals by choosing individuals in their organization to be Benefits Administrators. The portal shows how many of each benefit an organization has been allocated, and it's also where the benefits are activated (where required) and assigned.

Applying your knowledge in the exam:

- Remember that SA is a mandatory part of an Enterprise Agreement so even if the customer scenario doesn't mention Software Assurance specifically, you can assume that an EA customer has active SA on their licenses

Key SA Differences with the MPSA

As you know, the MPSA is a new licensing agreement and, as such, has a couple of differences from the other Volume Licensing agreements and several of them are in the area of Software Assurance so let's take a look at those now.

The first difference is the portal that is used to manage the SA benefits. The Volume Licensing Service Center (VLSC) is used for all of the programs except the MPSA which uses a brand new portal, the Microsoft Volume Licensing Center (MVLC).

The second difference is that benefits such as Training Vouchers don't need to be activated under the MPSA. Many of the existing benefits do need to be activated within VLSC but this has been removed in MVLC. As we go through the individual benefits I'll highlight where they need to be activated and you should assume this does not apply to benefits acquired through the MPSA.

And finally, there has been a change in how the amount of Planning Services, Training Vouchers and 24x7 Problem Resolution Support benefits are calculated. Outside of the MPSA there are various methods to work out a customer's allocation of these benefits, but within the MPSA they are all worked out via a much simpler points system.

New Version Rights

New Version Rights are probably the most well known of all the SA benefits: if an organization buys, for example, an Office Professional Plus license with SA then they're entitled to use any newer versions of Office released during the term of their agreement. If they haven't installed that newer version of Office by the time their agreement ends, even if they don't renew the agreement, they are still licensed for that version – as long as they have purchased perpetual Office licenses of course.

Applying your knowledge in the exam:

- Look out for particular business goals that specify that it's important for the organization to always have the latest version of the software available – perhaps there's a line of business application that relies on having the latest version of SQL Server deployed, for example

- It's significantly easier to manage an estate where all devices are running the same versions of a product, so look out for business goals that express a desire for easier management of client or server devices through a consistent set of products

- Watch out for statements telling you what the software refresh cycle of an organization is; if it's five years for example, benefits such as New Version Rights are not attractive and you may need to recommend an MPSA or Select Plus agreement without Software Assurance

- In the exam, as in real life, New Version Rights become even more attractive as the launch of a new product comes closer. So look out for an organization's concern that if they buy licenses now they won't be licensed for the new product that is scheduled to arrive in a couple of months' time; adding SA to their license purchase will overcome this objection

Step Up Licenses

Customers with Software Assurance are eligible to buy Step Up licenses – note that they don't actually receive them as an SA benefit automatically as part of their agreement. A Step Up license allows a customer to move from a lower edition of a product to a higher edition by just paying the difference in the License with SA price – this is the Step Up license price.

As an example, if a customer has a SQL Server Standard license and later needs to deploy SQL Server Enterprise edition, they need to acquire an Enterprise edition license. If they have no SA on the SQL Server Standard license then they need to purchase a new Enterprise edition license in the usual way. However, if they do have SA on the SQL Server Standard license then they can just purchase the Step Up license and thus will just pay the difference in L&SA prices, potentially saving a significant amount of money.

Another really good example of when Step Up licenses are useful is with Windows Server 2012 R2 since it allows a customer to move from Standard to Datacenter licenses as their virtualization needs grow.

Note that Step Up licenses were not available in the MPSA at its launch with SA in September 2014.

Applying your knowledge in the exam:

- Look out for business goals that indicate that an organization is unsure what edition of a particular product that they should deploy, but want to buy licenses now with the flexibility of choosing a different edition later

- If you see details of an organization which has already bought a product with SA and now realizes that they want to actually deploy a higher edition of the product, then this should lead you to recommend purchasing Step Up licenses

Microsoft Desktop Optimization Pack (MDOP)

As with Step Up licenses it's the right to purchase MDOP that is the SA benefit. The Microsoft Desktop Optimization Pack is a set of tools that organizations use to deploy and manage their desktops, perhaps the most well-known (and most used) of which is App-V, Microsoft's application virtualization tool.

It's a benefit that's specifically linked to purchases of Windows 8.1; if an organization has active SA on their Windows 8.1 Enterprise licenses allocated to their desktops then they're allowed to buy MDOP for those desktops.

It's worth noting that MDOP is actually a subscription – there are no perpetual versions of MDOP available – and thus it can only be used as long as the agreement is active.

Applying your knowledge in the exam:

- Look out for business goals that state the organization's desire to better manage and optimize their desktops, or even a requirement to acquire App-V which is only available as part of MDOP

Windows To Go

If you acquire a Windows 8.1 Enterprise license and add Software Assurance to it then you receive the rights to run Windows in a Windows To Go deployment. With Windows To Go, each employee is given a USB stick which contains their corporate desktop and when they insert it into a machine their personal desktop is available to them.

This is a way of rolling out standard desktops to users without having to set up a Virtual Desktop Infrastructure and you can imagine that it's attractive because of that. Technically, a Windows To Go USB stick can only be used in a device certified for Windows 7 or later whereas a VDI desktop can be delivered to a device that can't run Windows, like an iPad.

From a licensing perspective, it's licensed in exactly the same way as VDI desktops: the primary user of the device licensed with Windows + SA can use their Windows To Go desktop in any third party machine off the company premises and the Companion Subscription License can be used to license Windows for personal devices brought into the office.

Applying your knowledge in the exam:

- Look out for business goals that state the organization's desire to deploy corporate desktops for all users, and then decide if VDI or Windows To Go will be the best solution for the customer

- Remember that a Windows To Go USB stick can't be used in a device that can't run Windows so don't recommend it for delivering corporate desktops to non-Windows tablets for example

- Look out for business goals that state that users will bring their own devices onto the company premises to use their Windows To Go desktops. Remember that this scenario isn't covered under the main Windows + SA license and you'd need to recommend Companion Subscription Licenses to cover these devices

Windows Local Virtualization Rights

The Windows local virtualization rights benefit is aimed at developers and testers who need to have several different environments set up to work on different projects, and this SA benefit allows them to have up to 4 virtual machines running Windows 8.1 Enterprise locally on their device.

Applying your knowledge in the exam:

- You are less likely to have to pick out "local virtualization rights" as an answer than you are to state how many virtual machines this benefit allows to run locally, so look out for business goals that state that users need to work with multiple virtual machines and remember that this benefit allows 4 of these

Windows Enterprise Sideloading Rights

Enterprise Sideloading is the process of installing Windows Apps directly to a device without going through the Windows Store. You can imagine that this is ideal for organizations that want to build their own custom line of business apps and then distribute them directly to their devices since it would make no sense to make those apps publicly available through the Windows Store.

Although there have been some changes to how Windows Enterprise Sideloading Rights are acquired, you should assume for the purposes of the exam that they are a Software Assurance benefit for customers who acquire SA on their Windows licenses.

Applying your knowledge in the exam:

- You can imagine that you won't have a whole host of questions on this particular SA benefit, but do make sure that you can match it to a customer's need to install apps without going through the Windows Store and alternatively, to disregard it as a wrong answer with confidence

Enhanced Edition Rights

Enhanced Edition Rights is a relatively new SA benefit and is quite specialized. Essentially it allows a customer licensed with either Windows 8.1 Enterprise or Windows 8.1 Industry Enterprise with active SA to deploy either edition of Windows in any prior version. This quite nicely aligns the two flavors of Windows and the obvious benefit to the customer is that they have deployment flexibility.

Today, the Industry Enterprise edition contains all of the features in the regular Enterprise edition, with extra functionality useful for industry scenarios – so perhaps deploying Windows on specialist medical devices, for example.

Applying your knowledge in the exam:

- Check the infrastructure sections of the customer scenarios to see if they have any devices that the Industry editions of Windows would be suitable for as this may lead you to recommend this SA benefit for deployment flexibility

Enterprise Source Licensing Program

The Enterprise Source Licensing Program provides source code for most major releases and service packs of Windows client and server products, and its main purpose is to assist in the support and development of internally deployed applications on the Windows platform.

Customers must apply to join the program and there are two main criteria that they must meet: they must have an Enterprise Agreement or have committed to Software Assurance Membership through Select Plus or the MPSA on the Systems pool, and they must have a minimum of 10,000 Windows desktops.

Applying your knowledge in the exam:

- Remember that this benefit only applies to very large customers so bear that in mind if you decide to recommend it as a desired benefit in the exam

- It's also specific to customers who have SA on their Windows licenses through an EA or Select Plus/MPSA with SAM, so make sure that you only recommend it for customers in this situation

Virtual Desktop Access

The VDA SA benefit can be slightly confusing since there is a separate license available for purchase with exactly the same name – the Windows VDA license. VDA stands for Virtual Desktop Access and it's the licensing right that allows organizations to set up virtual desktops on their servers and to have their users access them from their desktop machines, and this infrastructure is of course known as a Virtual Desktop Infrastructure (VDI).

An ordinary Windows 8.1 Enterprise license purchased through a Volume Licensing agreement just allows the installation of Windows on the physical desktop device – it's only when you add SA that you get the added deployment flexibility of being allowed to create, store and run virtual desktops on a server.

Applying your knowledge in the exam:

- You'll see from the other benefits described in the following sections that if an organization wants to deploy virtual desktops in a Virtual Desktop Infrastructure then they absolutely need Software Assurance on their Windows licenses. So, use that as your trigger – if the business is interested in desktop virtualization, then you need to recommend SA on the Windows licenses. This is also a great piece of advice when you're talking to your real life customers about desktop virtualization

Companion Subscription License

A Companion Subscription License (CSL) may be purchased and assigned to a device which is licensed with Windows 8.1 Enterprise and SA. The primary user of that licensed device is then allowed to access Windows 8.1 Enterprise running in either a VDI or Windows To Go environment on up to 5 devices.

These devices may be any type of personally-owned device, used both on the corporate premises and outside of the office. They can also be a secondary, corporate-owned non x-86 device and again can be used anywhere.

Applying your knowledge in the exam:

- When you see a business goal of virtualizing desktops or deploying Windows To Go desktops you should have this SA benefit in your mind. Recommend it when there are already Windows + SA licenses on users' main devices but they want to bring in their own devices to access their corporate desktops, or when they have been assigned a secondary device – a tablet, for example

Windows Roaming Use Rights

Roaming Use Rights are available when a customer adds Software Assurance to Windows licenses. Organizations generally need Roaming Use Rights when they are making use of desktop virtualization. In a VDI environment the virtual desktops are stored on and run from a server, but each endpoint that the virtual desktop is being delivered to needs to be licensed for Windows. This obviously has the potential to be extremely expensive so Roaming Use Rights relax this condition and give the primary user of the device licensed with Windows + SA the rights to access a corporate desktop on a third party-owned device outside of the corporate premises.

Applying your knowledge in the exam:

- Since this SA benefit is very specific, look for a very specific set of business goals – the organization wants to allow access to virtual desktops (or Windows To Go desktops) on third party-owned devices outside of the corporate premises

- Don't forget that any virtual desktops are likely to consist of both Windows 8.1 and Office 2013, so the customer needs to purchase SA for both the Windows 8.1 and Office 2013 licenses if they want to deliver virtual desktops to third party-owned devices outside of the corporate premises

Windows Thin PC

The Windows Thin PC technology is aimed at organizations who want to move to a Virtual Desktop Infrastructure. Essentially, it allows an IT department to repurpose existing PCs as thin clients running a smaller footprint version of Windows, rather than having to buy new thin client devices. This allows an organization to try out VDI without extra hardware expense.

Windows Thin PC is available as an SA benefit to organizations adding SA to their Windows licenses in Select Plus, MPSA and Enterprise Agreements.

Applying your knowledge in the exam:

- Look out for business goals that state an organization's desire to evaluate desktop virtualization in a Virtual Desktop Infrastructure

- Remember that this feature can remove a cost barrier since the organization does not have to invest in new hardware, so if the business goals focus on worries about how much a VDI solution will cost, this is a good benefit to recommend

Office Multi-Language Pack

The Office Multi-Language Pack (MLP) is aimed at customers who need to deploy Office in multiple languages, since it enables them to deploy a single Office image with support for over 30 user interface languages. Users can switch languages for the interface elements (on-screen menus, for example) and also use the proofing tools (spelling and grammar checker, for example) of a language.

Customers must have Software Assurance on their Office licenses to be eligible for this benefit and, as long as they have acquired a perpetual license for Office, the rights to use the Office MLP persist even after SA has expired. Note that the Office Multi-Language Pack is one of the benefits that needs to be activated within VLSC.

Applying your knowledge in the exam:

- Look out for details about the organization that specify that they exist in several different locations – these are likely to be locations that very obviously use different languages, and may be a trigger for you to recommend the Office MLP

- Remember that the Office MLP is an SA benefit that persists after the SA expires (assuming the customer has a perpetual license for Office), so you should still recommend this SA benefit even if it is clear that the SA will not be renewed after the initial term

Office Online

Office Online used to be called the Office Web Apps but, actually, Office Online is a much better name since you don't actually install an app, you get access to online versions of Word, OneNote, PowerPoint and Excel through a browser. The experience is very similar to the familiar desktop products although there is less functionality available.

Access to Office Online is included in all of the Office 365 Plans we looked at earlier but it's only available as an SA benefit for Office licenses acquired through a Volume Licensing program. Specifically, the primary user of a device licensed with Office Standard, Office Professional Plus or Office for Mac Standard with Software Assurance can use Office Online for viewing and editing documents from any device.

Applying your knowledge in the exam:

- Look out for business goals that state that an organization wants a group of users to have a cost-effective way of viewing and editing Office documents from any device as this could lead to a recommendation for using Office Online

Home Use Program

The Home Use Program benefit is available to customers who purchase Software Assurance on qualifying Applications pool licenses. These qualifying products are Office Standard and Professional Plus, the individual Office components (Word, Excel etc.), and the two Office family products, Project and Visio. The users of a licensed device are then able to purchase a copy of the corresponding product for home use for installation on one home computer and one portable device. They may use this software as long as their organization's SA is active. One of the attractions of the Home Use Program is that it's a very cheap license to purchase and thus is an extremely cost-effective way of getting users to use the same product at home as they do at work.

The Home Use Program is another benefit which must be activated in VLSC, after which the administrator receives a Program Code which is shared with employees who purchase the software through the HUP Online Store.

Applying your knowledge in the exam:

- Look for business goals where the organization is deploying a new version of Office and they want to make the transition easier for users so that they're using the same products at home as they are at work

- Look out also for business goals relating to an HR director who's interested in giving his employees some additional benefits – it's perceived to be of value to employees to not have to purchase high-cost software for home use

- Also be on the lookout for business goals that state that end user productivity is important to the organization – the assumption being that users who use the same versions of products in both their work and home environments will be more productive with the tools

Office Roaming Use Rights

Roaming Use Rights are available when a customer adds Software Assurance to Office licenses. Organizations generally need Roaming Use Rights when they are making use of desktop virtualization. In a VDI environment the virtual desktops are stored on and run from a server, but each endpoint that the virtual desktop is being delivered to needs to be licensed for the desktop products – Windows 8.1 and Office 2013.

This obviously has the potential to be extremely expensive so Roaming Use Rights relax this condition and gives the primary user of the device licensed with Windows + SA and Office + SA the rights to access a corporate desktop on a third party-owned device outside of the corporate premises.

Roaming Use Rights are also useful when Office is installed on and run from a server in a Remote Desktop Services deployment. Again, every machine that accesses Office via RDS needs to be licensed with an individual Office license. However, if SA is added to the user's primary device, then that user may follow exactly the same rules above and access Office through RDS on any third party-owned device outside of the corporate premises.

Applying your knowledge in the exam:

- Since this SA benefit is very specific, look for a very specific set of business goals – the organization wants to allow access to certain products on third party-owned devices outside of the corporate premises. Don't forget that this could be through virtual desktops, or delivering Office via RDS

- Don't forget that any virtual desktops are likely to consist of both Windows 8.1 and Office 2013, so the customer needs to purchase SA for both the Windows 8.1 and Office 2013 licenses if they want to deliver virtual desktops to third party-owned devices outside of the corporate premises

Training Vouchers

Organizations are given an allocation of Training Vouchers dependent on the number of licenses they buy for products in the Systems pool (Windows 8.1) and the Applications pool (Office and the Office family products such as Visio and Project). As an example, within an Enterprise Agreement they would be allocated 30 Training Vouchers with a purchase of 2,500 Office Professional Plus 2013 licenses.

Training Vouchers are exchanged with qualified Microsoft Learning Partners for attendance on technical training courses – one voucher equates to one training day. There is a list of authorized training courses that vouchers can be exchanged for.

The Training Vouchers allocation is shown in the Volume Licensing portals and the Benefits Administrator is responsible for activating the benefit and then assigning the vouchers to individuals who book training courses with the Learning Partners directly. Note that the vouchers expire after 180 days after they have been created.

Training Vouchers are available as an SA benefit through the Enterprise Agreements and for Select Plus or MPSA customers who have SAM on the Applications or Systems pools.

Applying your knowledge in the exam:

- Look out for business goals that state that an organization wants to get their technical teams up to speed on certain products BEFORE they are deployed; benefits such as the 24x7 Problem Resolution Support, which we'll cover shortly, are typically associated with support AFTER the products are deployed

- If you're asked to pick out SA benefits that demonstrate a high return on investment, then strongly consider Training Vouchers; these are tangible, high value benefits that are easy to see the worth of

- Remember that Training Vouchers are not eligible for end user training, so disregard any answers that suggest that Training Vouchers could be exchanged for basic training to get end users up to speed on a new deployment of Office 2013, for example

- Also remember that Training Vouchers are not available through an MPSA or Select Plus agreement without SAM, so you can potentially disregard these programs as an option if you're recommending a Volume Licensing agreement for an organization where it's been established that Training Vouchers are important

E-Learning

It's good to consider E-Learning just after the Training Vouchers benefit since you need to be clear on the differences. Whilst the Training Vouchers benefit only applies to technical training, the E-Learning benefit is aimed at both technical users in the IT department and ordinary end users, offering online training courses across the three product pools – Systems, Applications, and Servers. Organizations receive access to the E-Learning courses in a particular pool dependent on the number of qualifying licenses with SA that they have purchased. Buying 575 Office Professional Plus licenses, for example, gives them access to all of the courses in the Applications pool for 575 users.

E-Learning is another benefit which must be activated, after which the administrator receives an Access Code which is shared with employees who can then use the code to access the training through the Microsoft Online Learning Portal.

Applying your knowledge in the exam:

- Look out for business goals where end users need access to training, or ALL users (both technical and end user) need access to training

- Look out for concerns where an organization is dubious about moving to the new versions of Office or Windows because of the perceived high cost of re-training users, since the E-Learning benefit can help overcome this concern

Planning Services

Planning Services are a collection of engagements offered by certified partners to help organizations to plan for, and thus to ultimately deploy, Microsoft products. Today there is a whole range of Planning Services for all the traditional on-premises products as well as Office 365 and Azure deployments.

Customers who purchase SA on qualifying Application and Server licenses receive an allocation of Planning Services days which the SA Benefits Administrator can see and exchange for vouchers in the Volume Licensing portals for spending with appropriate partners. Note that the vouchers expire after 180 days.

Customers who have unused Training Vouchers may convert them to Planning Services days at a ratio of 3:1, so three Training Vouchers may be exchanged for one Planning Services day. Note however, at the time that Software Assurance launched in the MPSA in September 2014 this conversion facility was not available in the MPSA.

Planning Services are available as an SA benefit through the Enterprise Agreements and for Select Plus and MPSA customers who have SAM on the Applications or Servers pools.

Applying your knowledge in the exam:

- Look for business goals that state a concern around planning for the deployment of a Microsoft product and a desire for external consultancy – skilling up internal staff would lead you towards recommending Training Vouchers rather than Planning Services

- Make sure that the business goals are referring to activities before deployment, rather than support after the deployment – where the Problem Resolution benefits will come into play

- Note that the Planning Services vouchers must be used for the partners to generate a deployment plan rather than for them to actually deploy the software, so check that the business goals requirement is for the planning phase before you select this benefit

System Center Global Service Monitor

System Center Global Service Monitor is a Microsoft cloud service that allows organizations to monitor the availability, performance and function of their external facing web applications. It's innovative since it can do this from multiple locations around the world by using Azure points of presence and thus simulating users across many geographies. As you would expect, the results integrate with the existing System Center 2012 R2 management console so that IT administrators can monitor all of their applications in one place.

Note that customers must specifically have Software Assurance on System Center 2012 R2 Server Management Licenses to be eligible for this benefit.

Applying your knowledge in the exam:

- Look out for organizations who have customers who use an important web application – it's going to be critical to know the state of that application and that's what this benefit can help with

- Don't get confused with the extra benefit that Server and Cloud Enrollment customers receive when they commit to the Core Infrastructure Component – that's the Cloud Management Benefit and allows customers to use System Center to manage Azure virtual machines

Extended Hotfix Support

The Extended Hotfix Support (EHFS) benefit is the second (and final) non-mainstream SA benefit that you need no great knowledge of for the exam, but again, knowing a little about it will mean that you can be sure that it is not the right answer to a Software Assurance question.

This benefit is aimed at customers who have older Microsoft products deployed and need an extra measure of support for them. When products go out of the Mainstream Support phase, non-security hotfixes are no longer automatically supplied by Microsoft, and the Extended Hotfix Support benefit allows a customer to request a specific product fix to extend the use of their legacy systems. Customers must have an existing Premier Support agreement with Microsoft to be eligible for this benefit, and if they want to be covered for the Applications or Systems pool they must have Software Assurance Membership on that pool if they are buying through an MPSA or Select Plus agreement.

Applying your knowledge in the exam:

- This benefit only applies to a very specific type of customer and will not be focused on in the exam. You should feel comfortable eliminating it as a possible answer in an SA question

24x7 Problem Resolution Support

The 24x7 Problem Resolution Support SA benefit provides assistance for organizations that are experiencing problems with Microsoft products. There are two types of support – through the web and via the phone. Organizations with SA on their server licenses purchased through both Select Plus/MPSA and Enterprise Agreements have unlimited web-based incidents. The number of phone incidents allocated to customers is based on how much they spend on SA (for Select Plus and Enterprise Agreements) or on a points system for MPSA.

Applying your knowledge in the exam:

- Look for business goals where an organization is worried about running into problems with their deployed software and getting support from Microsoft, as this benefit could alleviate this concern

- Watch out for particular mention of a requirement for out-of-hours support since that would lead you to recommend this SA benefit too

Fail-over Server Rights

SQL Server 2014 licenses with Software Assurance include fail-over rights. This means that SQL Server can be configured to provide redundancy so that if one server fails, its processing will be picked-up, recovered, and continued by another server without the need for additional licenses. There are two rules to bear in mind: the fail-over server must be a passive server, which means that it can't be running active SQL Server workloads or serving data to clients, and if the Core licensing model is being used then the fail-over server must have the same or fewer cores than the active server.

Applying your knowledge in the exam:

- For the products covered in the exam it is only SQL Server 2014 that has fail-over server benefits so this makes it easy to pick out when the benefit might be appropriate

Disaster Recovery Rights

This SA benefit is available when server products and their CALs (where available) are purchased with Software Assurance. It allows customers to deploy the same product on a "cold" – that is, a turned off – backup server for the purposes of disaster recovery; if the main server fails, then the organization is licensed to turn on the cold server and run the product from there without being concerned about license reassignment rules.

Applying your knowledge in the exam:

- Look for business goals which state a need for a disaster recovery option for server products

- Also look out for an organization's concerns about how much it costs to license backup servers; if they have cold backups, then buying SA is a much more cost-effective option than purchasing additional server licenses. However, do check that the backup solution is cold before you choose this option

Unlimited Virtualization Rights

Unlimited virtualization rights are only available for a handful of products and it's only SQL Server 2014 that you need to know about for the exam. If a physical server is licensed with SQL Server 2014 Enterprise Core licenses with Software Assurance then an unlimited number of virtual machines running SQL Server may be run on that physical server.

If a customer has a server farm with a high degree of virtualization with virtual machines that move between physical servers then this is a cost-effective way of licensing these products and adds considerably to the ease of management of the licensing of the virtual machines across the server farm.

Applying your knowledge in the exam:

- Be prepared to recommend the right number of licenses for a given server so that it is correctly licensed for unlimited virtualization

- Remember that (for the exam) it's only SQL Server 2014 that can be licensed for unlimited virtualization, so don't be tempted by answers that imply all products can be licensed for unlimited virtualization. Equally, remember that it's only the Enterprise edition of SQL Server 2014 that is eligible for this benefit

License Mobility within Server Farms

With all of the server applications licensed with the Server / CAL model that we looked at in the Product Licensing section, you assign a Server license to a physical server and that gives the rights to run the product either in the physical operating system environment or in a virtual machine. If you have a server farm where, say, a virtual machine running Exchange Server 2013 can move between physical servers this gives some licensing challenges due to the fact that a Server license cannot be reassigned to another physical server any sooner than every 90 days.

The License Mobility within Server Farms SA benefit relaxes this restriction so that, in effect, a license can follow a virtual machine around the server farm so that it's always correctly licensed.

The application servers – products such as Exchange, Lync and SharePoint – all have this right when SA is purchased with the license but it's also worth noting what products do NOT have these rights. The main ones to remember for the exam are the Core Infrastructure products – that's Windows Server 2012 R2 and System Center 2012 R2. When licenses are assigned in a server farm, they cannot be moved between servers any more frequently than every 90 days even with active Software Assurance.

Applying your knowledge in the exam:

- Look out for customers with a virtualized server farm since this SA benefit is likely to be a good recommendation
- Remember the products that do NOT have this benefit – the key ones being Windows Server 2012 R2 and System Center 2012 R2

License Mobility through SA

This SA benefit is aimed at organizations who want to take licenses that have been purchased through their Volume Licensing agreement and assign them to a Service Provider's hardware, so that the Service Provider can run the software as a managed service for the customer. This has been possible in the past, but only if the Service Provider's hardware was dedicated to the customer. Today, adding SA to the license purchase means that the licenses can be assigned to a Service Provider's SHARED hardware.

Be aware that a process does need to be followed – it's not simply a case of mentally assigning the licenses to the Service Provider's server farm. The License Verification Form must be completed and this gathers information such as the Service Provider and the number of licenses that are being assigned, and then it's sent to Microsoft to be verified.

This SA benefit is typically available when SA is added to server product licenses and customers must purchase SA on the CALs as well as the server licenses. Not all servers are eligible for this benefit, the most notable of which is Windows Server 2012 R2 which must stay assigned to an on-premises server. You can find out which products are eligible for this benefit by looking in the Product Use Rights document.

Right back in the Azure section in part 2 of this book we looked at how virtual machines are licensed in Azure and saw that a Windows Server virtual machine could be set up and paid for on a consumption basis. License Mobility through SA means that you can assign SQL Server licenses to that Windows VM to run SQL Server there. However, an alternative would be to buy a SQL Server VM in Azure which includes all the licenses and is again paid for on a consumption basis. If organizations have long-term SQL servers that they want to move to the cloud they would use the first method, and if they have short-term workloads it would be more cost-effective to use the second method.

Applying your knowledge in the exam:

- Look for business goals that reflect an organization's desire to use Service Provider's shared hardware to scale their business solutions

- The Service Provider's hardware could be referred to as the "Public Cloud" and the organization's own infrastructure as the "Private Cloud" so use those terms as triggers to think about this benefit

- Remember that Windows Server 2012 R2 does not have this SA benefit so don't get carried away and recommend that a customer assign these licenses to a Service Provider

- You may need to recommend how a customer licenses a particular server for SQL in the cloud: if it's a long-term workload then recommend assigning licenses to an Azure Windows Server VM, if it's a short-term workload then recommend buying a full Azure SQL virtual machine

- Make sure you're clear on the differences between the "License Mobility through SA" benefit and the "License Mobility within Server Farms" one so that you can recommend the correct benefit from a list

Software Assurance Revision Cards

The following pages show the Revision Cards for the Software Assurance benefits where you'll find each benefit with a description. They are arranged in categories of benefits: General SA benefits, Windows Deployment benefits, Virtual Desktop Infrastructure benefits, Office Deployment benefits, Training and Support benefits, and Server Deployment benefits. As well as this making it easier for you to remember them for the exam, it's also a great way to talk to customers about them; if you focus on a specific area of benefits rather than trying to explain all of them it will be much easier for your customer to digest the benefits that may be of particular interest to them.

At the end there's a final card reminding you of the benefits that are not available to Select Plus or MPSA customers unless they sign up for Software Assurance Membership, and the specific benefits that need to be activated within the VLSC.

Revision Card 30:
General SA Benefits

Benefit Name	Description
New Version Rights	New Version Rights allow an organization to use a newer version of a product released during the term of their agreement
Step Up Licenses	Step Up licenses allow organizations to move from a lower edition of a product to a higher edition by just paying the difference in the License with SA price

Revision Card 31:
Windows Deployment SA Benefits

Benefit Name	Description
Microsoft Desktop Optimization Pack (MDOP)	Organizations that have SA on their Windows 8.1 Enterprise licenses can buy MDOP for those desktops. MDOP is a collection of tools to help organizations deploy and manage their desktops, the most common of which is App-V, the desktop virtualization tool
Windows To Go	Windows To Go allows organizations to deploy corporate desktops via a USB stick
Windows Local Virtualization Rights	The local virtualization rights allow a user to install and use up to four virtual machines running Windows 8.1 Enterprise on his local device
Enterprise Sideloading Rights	Enterprise Sideloading is the process of installing Windows Apps directly to a device without going through the Windows Store
Enhanced Edition Rights	Enhanced Edition Rights allow a customer licensed with either Windows 8.1 Enterprise or Windows 8.1 Industry Enterprise with active SA to deploy either edition of Windows in any prior version
Enterprise Source Licensing Program	The Enterprise Source Licensing Program gives access to Windows source code to support applications deployed on the Windows platform

Revision Card 32:
Virtual Desktop Infrastructure SA Benefits

Benefit Name	Description
Virtual Desktop Access	VDA allows organizations to create, store and run virtual desktops on a server in a Virtual Desktop Infrastructure
Companion Subscription License	A Companion Subscription License (CSL) may be purchased and assigned to a device which is licensed with Windows 8.1 Enterprise and SA. The primary user of that licensed device is then allowed to access Windows 8.1 Enterprise running in either a VDI or Windows To Go environment on up to 5 devices in any location
Windows Roaming Use Rights	Windows Roaming Use Rights allow the primary user of a device licensed with Windows 8.1 Enterprise and SA to access a virtual desktop running Windows on any third party-owned device outside the office
Windows Thin PC	Windows Thin PC enables organizations to repurpose existing PCs as thin clients to access a Virtual Desktop Infrastructure

Revision Card 33:
Office Deployment SA Benefits

Benefit Name	Description
Office Multi-Language Pack (MLP)	The Office MLP enables organizations to deploy a single Office image with support for over 30 user interface languages. This benefit persists after SA expires on perpetual licenses
Office Online	Office Online gives access to online versions of Word, OneNote, PowerPoint and Excel through a browser
Home Use Program	The Home Use Program allows end users to purchase Office for use on their home PCs
Office Roaming Use Rights	Office Roaming Use Rights allow the primary user of a device licensed with Office Standard/Professional Plus 2013 and SA to access a virtual desktop running Office on any third party-owned device outside the office, or to access Office delivered via RDS

Revision Card 34:
Training and Support SA Benefits

Benefit Name	Description
Training Vouchers	Training Vouchers are exchanged with Microsoft Learning Partners for technical training courses
E-Learning	The E-Learning SA benefit allows access to online training courses aimed at both technical users and end users
Planning Services	Planning Services are delivered by certified partners to help organizations to plan for the deployment of Microsoft products
System Center Global Service Monitor	System Center Global Service Monitor is a Microsoft cloud service that extends application monitoring capabilities beyond an internal network
Extended Hotfix Support (EHFS)	Customers with an existing support agreement can use this benefit to request a product fix for a product out of Mainstream Support
24x7 Problem Resolution Support	This SA benefit provides web-based or phone support to solve problems relating to Microsoft products

Revision Card 35:
Server Deployment SA Benefits

Benefit Name	Description
Fail-over Server Rights	Only applicable to SQL Server, this means that SQL Server can be configured to provide redundancy so that if one server fails, its processing will be picked-up, recovered, and continued by another server without the need for additional licenses
Disaster Recovery Rights	Server (and CAL) licenses covered with SA allow customers to deploy the software on a cold backup server for the purposes of disaster recovery
Unlimited Virtualization Rights	Unlimited Virtualization Rights are granted to SQL Server 2014 when a physical server is completely licensed with Enterprise Core licenses with Software Assurance
License Mobility within Server Farms	This SA benefit relaxes the 90 day license reassignment rule so that virtual machines may move freely around a server farm and the server licenses may be reassigned as required
License Mobility through SA	License Mobility through SA allows an organization to assign server licenses to a Service Provider's shared hardware so that the software may be run there as a managed service. The License Verification Form must be completed as part of the process

Revision Card 36:
SA Benefits Exceptions

Benefits	Exception
Training Vouchers Planning Services	Only available to MPSA and Select Plus customers if Software Assurance Membership (SAM) is taken
Training Vouchers **H**ome Use Program **E**-Learning **O**ffice Multi-Language Pack	Benefits that need to be activated in VLSC. Remember Theo!

Recap Questions and Answers

Use these Recap Questions to see how much you know about the Software Assurance benefits. If you find any areas that you need to go over you can review the relevant topic in this section of the book. As usual, you'll find a couple of questions on each page with the answers when you turn over.

Questions 1 – 3

1. Blue Lamp Ideas are considering deploying Exchange Server but do not have any in-house IT expertise around the installation and setup of Exchange Server. If they purchase Software Assurance with their Exchange Server licenses through their Enterprise Agreement, what SA benefits could help them with this? Choose two answers.

   a) Cold Backups for Disaster Recovery
   b) Training Vouchers
   c) Step Up licenses
   d) Planning Services

2. The Papaya Hire Company are undergoing a desktop virtualization project and as part of it, want to allow their employees to access their virtual desktops running Windows 8.1 Enterprise and Office Professional Plus 2013 from an end user-owned PC at home. They are intending to purchase their Windows and Office licenses with SA through an MPSA. What included SA benefit will allow them to deploy Windows and Office in this way?

   a) They need Roaming Use Rights but the MPSA does not include them
   b) Roaming Use Rights
   c) They need Virtual Desktop Access but the MPSA does not include this benefit
   d) Virtual Desktop Access rights

3. Cyan Ida's Pharmacy have an Enterprise Agreement. Where should they go to manage and activate their SA benefits?

   a) MVLS
   b) eOpen
   c) OVSA
   d) VLSC

Answers 1 – 3

1. Blue Lamp Ideas are considering deploying Exchange Server but do not have any in-house IT expertise around the installation and setup of Exchange Server. If they purchase Software Assurance with their Exchange Server licenses through their Enterprise Agreement, what SA benefits could help them with this? Choose two answers.
    a) Cold Backups for Disaster Recovery
    b) **Training Vouchers** ✓
    c) Step Up licenses
    d) **Planning Services** ✓

2. The Papaya Hire Company are undergoing a desktop virtualization project and as part of it, want to allow their employees to access their virtual desktops running Windows 8.1 Enterprise and Office Professional Plus 2013 from an end user-owned PC at home. They are intending to purchase their Windows and Office licenses with SA through an MPSA. What included SA benefit will allow them to deploy Windows and Office in this way?
    a) They need Roaming Use Rights but the MPSA does not include them
    b) **Roaming Use Rights** ✓
    c) They need Virtual Desktop Access but the MPSA does not include this benefit
    d) Virtual Desktop Access

3. Cyan Ida's Pharmacy have an Enterprise Agreement. Where should they go to manage and activate their SA benefits?
    a) MVLS
    b) eOpen
    c) OVSA
    d) **VLSC** ✓

Questions 4 – 6

4. The Cobalt Bolt Company are concerned about supporting their IT department once they have deployed SharePoint Server. They have Software Assurance on all of their licenses. Which of the following benefits is likely to prove most beneficial to the IT department?

    a) 24x7 Problem Resolution Support
    b) Training Vouchers
    c) E-Learning
    d) Extended Hotfix Support

5. Goldfinger Food have always deployed their software on-premises and managed it themselves. They are now considering using a Service Provider's shared hardware for a new deployment of SQL Server. They have been told that they should include SA on their new SQL licenses. Why have they been told this?

    a) This is an error – as long as they purchase the licenses through a Volume Licensing agreement then they can deploy the software either on their own hardware or on a Service Provider's
    b) They need the Roaming Use Rights SA benefit
    c) They need the License Mobility through SA benefit
    d) They need the Step Up Licenses SA benefit

6. Blacken White Solicitors have offices throughout Europe and need to deploy Office in multiple languages. Which SA benefit will help them achieve this?

    a) Office Multi-User Language Rights
    b) Office Online
    c) Office MLP
    d) Office Roaming Use Rights

4. The Cobalt Bolt Company are concerned about supporting their IT department once they have deployed SharePoint Server. They have Software Assurance on all of their licenses. Which of the following benefits is likely to prove most beneficial to the IT department?

   a) **24x7 Problem Resolution Support** ✓
   b) Training Vouchers
   c) E-Learning
   d) Extended Hotfix Support

5. Goldfinger Food have always deployed their software on-premises and managed it themselves. They are now considering using a Service Provider's shared hardware for a new deployment of SQL Server. They have been told that they should include SA on their new SQL licenses. Why have they been told this?

   a) This is an error – as long as they purchase the licenses through a Volume Licensing agreement then they can deploy the software either on their own hardware or on a Service Provider's
   b) They need the Roaming Use Rights SA benefit
   c) **They need the License Mobility through SA benefit** ✓
   d) They need the Step Up Licenses SA benefit

6. Blacken White Solicitors have offices throughout Europe and need to deploy Office in multiple languages. Which SA benefit will help them achieve this?

   a) Office Multi-User Language Rights
   b) Office Online
   c) **Office MLP** ✓
   d) Office Roaming Use Rights

Questions 7 – 9

7. Aisle of White Paints want to deploy their applications using Microsoft's application virtualization product – App-V. How should they acquire App-V?

   a) They should purchase SA with their Windows licenses since this will then give them rights to MDOP which includes App-V

   b) They should purchase SA with their Windows licenses since this will give them rights to Windows Enterprise edition which includes App-V

   c) They should purchase SA with their Windows licenses since this will give them Roaming Use Rights and thus the right to deploy App-V

   d) They should purchase SA with their Windows licenses since they are then able to purchase MDOP subscriptions which include App-V

8. Cerise Estate Management have a number of apps that they have built to support internal processes. They want to deploy these to their users' devices without having to go through the Windows Store. What SA benefit will assist them?

   a) Enterprise Sideloading Rights

   b) Rights to purchase MDOP

   c) VDA

   d) Enhanced Edition Rights

9. Peach Snaps Cameras are concerned about the task of training up their end users as they move to Office Professional Plus 2013, purchasing licenses through an Enterprise Agreement. What SA benefit may help them?

   a) Training Vouchers

   b) E-Learning

   c) Home Use Program

   d) MDOP

7. Aisle of White Paints want to deploy their applications using Microsoft's application virtualization product – App-V. How should they acquire App-V?

    a) They should purchase SA with their Windows licenses since this will then give them rights to MDOP which includes App-V

    b) They should purchase SA with their Windows licenses since this will give them rights to Windows Enterprise edition which includes App-V

    c) They should purchase SA with their Windows licenses since this will give them Roaming Use Rights and thus the right to deploy App-V

    d) They should purchase SA with their Windows licenses since they are then able to purchase MDOP subscriptions which include App-V ✓

8. Cerise Estate Management have a number of apps that they have built to support internal processes. They want to deploy these to their users' devices without having to go through the Windows Store. What SA benefit will assist them?

    a) Enterprise Sideloading Rights ✓

    b) Rights to purchase MDOP

    c) VDA

    d) Enhanced Edition Rights

9. Peach Snaps Cameras are concerned about the task of training up their end users as they move to Office Professional Plus 2013, purchasing licenses through an Enterprise Agreement. What SA benefit may help them?

    a) Training Vouchers

    b) E-Learning ✓

    c) Home Use Program

    d) MDOP

Questions 10 – 11

10. The IT manager at Ultramarine Swim Wear is planning for a Windows Server deployment. He needs to order licenses this month but is currently unsure as to whether Windows Standard or Datacenter edition is the right choice for him. Which of the following statements represents the best advice to him?

   a) He should buy a Windows Standard license with SA so that he gets License Mobility rights meaning that he can deploy a higher edition and then pay the difference in price if that edition is still in use at the end of the agreement

   b) As long as he purchases through a Volume Licensing program he should just buy a Windows Standard license – he can purchase a Step Up license at any time to move to Windows Datacenter edition

   c) He should buy a Windows Standard license with SA so that he can step up to Windows Datacenter edition at just the difference in L&SA price

   d) He should buy a Windows Standard license with SA since this gives rights to Datacenter edition

11. Scarlet Key Cutters are looking to implement a disaster recovery infrastructure for their latest deployment project. Which of the following represents the best advice to them?

   a) They should add SA to their license purchases so that they get Disaster Recovery Rights

   b) They should add SA to their license purchases so that they get rights to Step Up licenses meaning that they can purchase additional licenses for disaster recovery servers at a discount

   c) They should buy licenses for both the production servers and the disaster recovery servers

   d) They should add SA to their license purchases so that they get rights to the Enterprise editions of the product which include Disaster Recovery Rights

10. The IT manager at Ultramarine Swim Wear is planning for a Windows Server deployment. He needs to order licenses this month but is currently unsure as to whether Windows Standard or Datacenter edition is the right choice for him. Which of the following statements represents the best advice to him?

    a) He should buy a Windows Standard license with SA so that he gets License Mobility rights meaning that he can deploy a higher edition and then pay the difference in price if that edition is still in use at the end of the agreement

    b) As long as he purchases through a Volume Licensing program he should just buy a Windows Standard license – he can purchase a Step Up license at any time to move to Windows Datacenter edition

    c) **He should buy a Windows Standard license with SA so that he can step up to Windows Datacenter edition at just the difference in L&SA price** ✓

    d) He should buy a Windows Standard license with SA since this gives rights to Datacenter edition

11. Scarlet Key Cutters are looking to implement a disaster recovery infrastructure for their latest deployment project. Which of the following represents the best advice to them?

    a) **They should add SA to their license purchases so that they get Disaster Recovery Rights** ✓

    b) They should add SA to their license purchases so that they get rights to Step Up licenses meaning that they can purchase additional licenses for disaster recovery servers at a discount

    c) They should buy licenses for both the production servers and the disaster recovery servers

    d) They should add SA to their license purchases so that they get rights to the Enterprise editions of the product which include Disaster Recovery Rights

Questions 12 – 14

12. Taupe Telecoms have a mixed environment with devices running either Windows 8.1 Enterprise or Windows 8.1 Industry Enterprise editions. They want the flexibility to deploy either of these editions. What SA benefit will allow them to do this?

    a) Enterprise Sideloading Rights
    b) Enhanced Edition Rights
    c) Windows Thin PC
    d) Roaming Use Rights

13. Pink Champagne Limousines have deployed a Virtual Desktop Infrastructure and now want to allow users to bring their devices in from home and access their Windows desktops from those devices. What is the most cost-effective way of licensing this for Windows?

    a) Enterprise Sideloading Rights
    b) Companion Subscription License
    c) MDOP
    d) Roaming Use Rights

14. The HR Manager at Spring Green Grocers is interested in knowing if there are any SA benefits that will help users' productivity. What would you recommend?

    a) Deploying Windows 8.1 Enterprise with the EaseOfUse functionality turned on
    b) Allowing users to use multiple virtual desktops
    c) Buying users software for home use through the Home Use Program
    d) Deploying user desktops using MDOP

12. Taupe Telecoms have a mixed environment with devices running either Windows 8.1 Enterprise or Windows 8.1 Industry Enterprise editions. They want the flexibility to deploy either of these editions. What SA benefit will allow them to do this?

    a) Enterprise Sideloading Rights
    b) **Enhanced Edition Rights** ✓
    c) Windows Thin PC
    d) Roaming Use Rights

13. Pink Champagne Limousines have deployed a Virtual Desktop Infrastructure and now want to allow users to bring their devices in from home and access their Windows desktops from those devices. What is the most cost-effective way of licensing this for Windows?

    a) Enterprise Sideloading Rights
    b) **Companion Subscription License** ✓
    c) MDOP
    d) Roaming Use Rights

14. The HR Manager at Spring Green Grocers is interested in knowing if there are any SA benefits that will help users' productivity. What would you recommend?

    a) Deploying Windows 8.1 Enterprise with the EaseOfUse functionality turned on
    b) Allowing users to use multiple virtual desktops
    c) **Buying users software for home use through the Home Use Program** ✓
    d) Deploying user desktops using MDOP

Questions 15 – 17

15. Mauve Stoves, a 1,350-seat organization, want to train their technical team and are particularly interested in the Training Vouchers SA benefit. Which licensing agreement would you recommend that Mauve Stoves acquire their licenses through?

    a) Through a Select Plus agreement as long as they have SA on more than 50% of their licenses
    b) Through an Open agreement with SA
    c) Through an MPSA
    d) Through an Enterprise Agreement

16. World of Magnolia want to ensure that their IT support team feel fully supported when they have deployed SharePoint Server. Which SA benefit will be useful to them?

    a) Training Vouchers
    b) 24x7 Problem Resolution Support
    c) Disaster Recovery Rights
    d) Planning Services

17. The IT Manager at Powderblue Pottery is not sure whether his upcoming SQL Server deployment will require SQL Server Standard or SQL Server Enterprise edition. How will SA help him in this dilemma?

    a) SA allows a one-time edition swap
    b) SA allows him to deploy any edition of a product
    c) SA allows him to buy Step Up licenses
    d) SA allows him to spread payments

15. Mauve Stoves, a 1,350-seat organization, want to train their technical team and are particularly interested in the Training Vouchers SA benefit. Which licensing agreement would you recommend that Mauve Stoves acquire their licenses through?

    a) Through a Select Plus agreement as long as they have SA on more than 50% of their licenses
    b) Through an Open agreement with SA
    c) Through an MPSA
    d) Through an Enterprise Agreement ✓

16. World of Magnolia want to ensure that their IT support team feel fully supported when they have deployed SharePoint Server. Which SA benefit will be useful to them?

    a) Training Vouchers
    b) 24x7 Problem Resolution Support ✓
    c) Disaster Recovery Rights
    d) Planning Services

17. The IT Manager at Powderblue Pottery is not sure whether his upcoming SQL Server deployment will require SQL Server Standard or SQL Server Enterprise edition. How will SA help him in this dilemma?

    a) SA allows a one-time edition swap
    b) SA allows him to deploy any edition of a product
    c) SA allows him to buy Step Up licenses ✓
    d) SA allows him to spread payments

Questions 18 – 20

18. The Pink Pillow Shop are about to start a project to deploy SharePoint Server 2013. Their technical team need some assistance in working out the best way to deploy this product in their organization. What SA benefit is likely to be a good fit for them?

    a) Training Vouchers
    b) Planning Services
    c) E-Learning
    d) Deployment Services

19. Periwinkle Packaging Solutions are keen on trialing a Virtual Desktop Infrastructure and want eventually to deploy it using thin client hardware. However, the hardware cost is currently delaying the trial. What SA benefit could you recommend to help this project?

    a) VDA
    b) Windows Thin PC
    c) MDOP
    d) Roaming Use Rights

20. There are a team of developers at The Olive Oil Drum Company who want to be able to run Windows in virtual machines installed on their laptops to simulate different companies' test environments. They know that the Windows 8.1 local virtualization rights SA benefit will allow them to do this, but how many virtual machines will they be able to run on each machine?

    a) 1
    b) 2
    c) 4
    d) Unlimited

18. The Pink Pillow Shop are about to start a project to deploy SharePoint Server 2013. Their technical team need some assistance in working out the best way to deploy this product in their organization. What SA benefit is likely to be a good fit for them?

    a) Training Vouchers
    b) **Planning Services** ✓
    c) E-Learning
    d) Deployment Services

19. Periwinkle Packaging Solutions are keen on trialing a Virtual Desktop Infrastructure and want eventually to deploy it using thin client hardware. However, the hardware cost is currently delaying the trial. What SA benefit could you recommend to help this project?

    a) VDA
    b) **Windows Thin PC** ✓
    c) MDOP
    d) Roaming Use Rights

20. There are a team of developers at The Olive Oil Drum Company who want to be able to run Windows in virtual machines installed on their laptops to simulate different companies' test environments. They know that the Windows 8.1 local virtualization rights SA benefit will allow them to do this, but how many virtual machines will they be able to run on each machine?

    a) 1
    b) 2
    c) **4** ✓
    d) Unlimited

Questions 21 – 23

21. The HR manager at Sienna Blenders has seen that her organization has an allocation of 35 Training Vouchers and wants to know what sort of training they can be used for. Which of the following would she be allowed to use the vouchers for?

    a) Technical training – how to deploy SQL Server, for example
    b) End user training – Excel basics, for example
    c) Soft skills training – time management, for example
    d) Any of the above

22. The IT manager at The Mala Kite Shop is considering a desktop virtualization project, and he has already purchased Software Assurance on all Windows and Office licenses. Which of the following SA benefits will be of interest to him as he plans this virtualization project? Choose two answers.

    a) E-Learning
    b) Virtual Desktop Access (VDA)
    c) Windows and Office Roaming Use Rights
    d) Step Up licenses

23. Xanthic Tractors have added MDOP to their Enterprise Agreement. For how long will they be licensed to use the MDOP tools?

    a) Licenses purchased through an Enterprise Agreement are perpetual licenses so they will be able to use these tools for ever
    b) MDOP licenses are subscription licenses so they will be able to use the tools as long as the agreement is active
    c) MDOP licenses are sold for periods of five years and the customer can choose whether or not to renew the licenses at the end of the five year period
    d) MDOP can only be purchased through an Enterprise Subscription Agreement

Answers 21 – 23

21. The HR manager at Sienna Blenders has seen that her organization has an allocation of 35 Training Vouchers and wants to know what sort of training they can be used for. Which of the following would she be allowed to use the vouchers for?

   a) **Technical training – how to deploy SQL Server, for example** ✓
   b) End user training – Excel basics, for example
   c) Soft skills training – time management, for example
   d) Any of the above

22. The IT manager at The Mala Kite Shop is considering a desktop virtualization project, and he has already purchased Software Assurance on all Windows and Office licenses. Which of the following SA benefits will be of interest to him as he plans this virtualization project? Choose two answers.

   a) E-Learning
   b) **Virtual Desktop Access (VDA)** ✓
   c) **Windows and Office Roaming Use Rights** ✓
   d) Step Up licenses

23. Xanthic Tractors have added MDOP to their Enterprise Agreement. For how long will they be licensed to use the MDOP tools?

   a) Licenses purchased through an Enterprise Agreement are perpetual licenses so they will be able to use these tools for ever
   b) **MDOP licenses are subscription licenses so they will be able to use the tools as long as the agreement is active** ✓
   c) MDOP licenses are sold for periods of five years and the customer can choose whether or not to renew the licenses at the end of the five year period
   d) MDOP can only be purchased through an Enterprise Subscription Agreement

Questions 24 – 26

24. Maroon Balloons have a virtualized server farm and want to make sure that they license it in the most efficient way. What SA benefit is going to be of particular use to them?

    a) License Mobility through SA
    b) Licensing Mobility within Server Farms
    c) Disaster Recover Rights
    d) Fail-over Server Rights

25. The IT team at Vermilion Jewellers have identified that 20% of their help desk tickets are associated with problems regarding file compatibility amongst their users' documents. How could purchasing SA on their Office licenses over the years have helped them to overcome these issues?

    a) SA allows organizations to install the latest version of a product so that all users can be deployed on the same version
    b) SA gives access to document viewers so that users would always be able to read documents, regardless of what version of a product they were created with
    c) SA gives access to Version Deployment Accessibility (VDA) rights so that all users can be deployed on the same version
    d) SA allows organizations to spread the payments for their licenses so that they can afford to purchase newer versions of products as needed

26. Tangerine Truckers are keen to virtualize their desktops and run them from a server. What SA benefit will allow them to do this?

    a) VDA
    b) VDI
    c) MDOP
    d) Roaming Use Rights

24. Maroon Balloons have a virtualized server farm and want to make sure that they license it in the most efficient way. What SA benefit is going to be of particular use to them?

    a) License Mobility through SA
    b) Licensing Mobility within Server Farms ✓
    c) Disaster Recover Rights
    d) Fail-over Server Rights

25. The IT team at Vermilion Jewellers have identified that 20% of their help desk tickets are associated with problems regarding file compatibility amongst their users' documents. How could purchasing SA on their Office licenses over the years have helped them to overcome these issues?

    a) SA allows organizations to install the latest version of a product so that all users can be deployed on the same version ✓
    b) SA gives access to document viewers so that users would always be able to read documents, regardless of what version of a product they were created with
    c) SA gives access to Version Deployment Accessibility (VDA) rights so that all users can be deployed on the same version
    d) SA allows organizations to spread the payments for their licenses so that they can afford to purchase newer versions of products as needed

26. Tangerine Truckers are keen to virtualize their desktops and run them from a server. What SA benefit will allow them to do this?

    a) VDA ✓
    b) VDI
    c) MDOP
    d) Roaming Use Rights

Questions 27 – 30

27. The IT Manager at Copper Feel Fabrics has a server which he wants to license for unlimited virtualization for SQL Server 2014 Enterprise edition. The server has four processors each with four cores. What licenses should he purchase?

   a) 8 Enterprise Core licenses
   b) 16 Enterprise Core licenses with SA
   c) 8 Enterprise Core licenses with SA
   d) 4 Enterprise Processor licenses with SA

28. Where should an MPSA customer go to manage SA benefits?

   a) MVLC
   b) VLSC
   c) SABC
   d) SASC

29. Amaranth Antiques want to roll out corporate desktops to all of their users by giving them a USB stick. What SA benefit gives them the right to do this?

   a) Virtual Desktop Access
   b) Windows To Go
   c) License Mobility through SA
   d) Roaming Use Rights

30. Which SA benefit allows users to view and edit documents through a browser?

   a) Office Web Apps
   b) MDOP
   c) Roaming Use Rights
   d) Office Online

27. The IT Manager at Copper Feel Fabrics has a server which he wants to license for unlimited virtualization for SQL Server 2014 Enterprise edition. The server has four processors each with four cores. What licenses should he purchase?

    a) 8 Enterprise Core licenses
    b) 16 Enterprise Core licenses with SA ✓
    c) 8 Enterprise Core licenses with SA
    d) 4 Enterprise Processor licenses with SA

28. Where should an MPSA customer go to manage SA benefits?

    a) MVLC ✓
    b) VLSC
    c) SABC
    d) SASC

29. Amaranth Antiques want to roll out corporate desktops to all of their users by giving them a USB stick. What SA benefit gives them the right to do this?

    a) Virtual Desktop Access
    b) Windows To Go ✓
    c) License Mobility through SA
    d) Roaming Use Rights

30. Which SA benefit allows users to view and edit documents through a browser?

    a) Office Web Apps
    b) MDOP
    c) Roaming Use Rights
    d) Office Online ✓

Questions 31 – 34

31. Which editions of SQL Server 2014 receive unlimited virtualization rights when SA is added to the license?
    a) Standard and Enterprise Core licenses
    b) All editions of SQL Server 2014
    c) Enterprise Core licenses
    d) Enterprise Core and Server licenses

32. What is the only product that has Fail-over Server Rights as an SA benefit?
    a) SQL Server 2014
    b) Windows Server 2012 R2
    c) System Center 2012 R2
    d) BizTalk Server 2013 R2

33. Which of the following products does NOT have License Mobility within Server Farms even with active SA?
    a) SQL Server 2014
    b) Windows Server 2012 R2
    c) SharePoint Server 2013
    d) CRM Server 2013

34. Staff at Coff E-Learning Solutions frequently work at third party-owned devices outside of their corporate premises to access a VDI desktop running Windows 8.1 and Office Professional Plus 2013. Which of the following SA benefits allows them to do this?
    a) Roaming Use Rights
    b) Virtual Desktop Access
    c) Enhanced Edition Rights
    d) Windows Thin PC

Answers 31 – 34

31. Which editions of SQL Server 2014 receive unlimited virtualization rights when SA is added to the license?
    a) Standard and Enterprise Core licenses
    b) All editions of SQL Server 2014
    c) Enterprise Core licenses ✓
    d) Enterprise Core and Server licenses

32. What is the only product that has Fail-over Server Rights as an SA benefit?
    a) SQL Server 2014 ✓
    b) Windows Server 2012 R2
    c) System Center 2012 R2
    d) BizTalk Server 2013 R2

33. Which of the following products does NOT have License Mobility within Server Farms even with active SA?
    a) SQL Server 2014
    b) Windows Server 2012 R2 ✓
    c) SharePoint Server 2013
    d) CRM Server 2013

34. Staff at Coff E-Learning Solutions frequently work at third party-owned devices outside of their corporate premises to access a VDI desktop running Windows 8.1 and Office Professional Plus 2013. Which of the following SA benefits allows them to do this?
    a) Roaming Use Rights ✓
    b) Virtual Desktop Access
    c) Enhanced Edition Rights
    d) Windows Thin PC

PART 5: LICENSING TOOLS AND RESOURCES

There are a number of tools and resources that are useful in real life and that you need to be familiar with for the exam. This section covers topics such as the Volume Licensing portals, product activation, license use rights, and tools such as explore.ms and eAgreements.

If you are already familiar with these tools and resources, why not skip to the Recap Questions on page 286 and test yourself?

Volume Licensing Service Center (VLSC)

If customers have purchased licenses through a Select Plus or Enterprise Agreement (or, in fact, through any of the small business agreements) then the Volume Licensing Service Center is a key portal to manage all aspects of their organization's licensing. Note that if a customer has purchased licenses through the MPSA then they use the Microsoft Volume Licensing Center (MVLC) which is covered in the next section.

We have already mentioned the Volume Licensing Service Center (VLSC) site in connection with Software Assurance, as it's the place where customers go to manage, activate and consume their SA benefits. Organizations assign Benefits Administrators who are responsible for tasks such as allocating Training Vouchers to individuals, for example.

However, VLSC has many other uses as it's the single place where organizations can access all of their licensing information and it's often used by people who work in procurement or Software Asset Management teams. These people can see all of the Volume Licensing agreements associated with their organization and the licenses that have been purchased through them, making it more straightforward to manage licenses throughout the whole organization.

VLSC is also a key site for technical staff for two main reasons. Firstly, it's the site where a deployment team would go to download the products that they have purchased licenses for. Note that although all of Microsoft's business software is available to download it's only for the current and immediately prior versions of products – often referred to as N and N-1 versions. The other thing to point out is that VLSC gives access to on-premises software but not, for example, Office 365 ProPlus which is downloaded from the Office 365 site.

Secondly, it's where IT administrators will find the necessary Volume License Keys to activate software, and we'll look at some specifics on this shortly.

All customers with a Volume Licensing agreement have access to VLSC and they can give their partners access if they want assistance in managing their agreement. The site is accessed at: www.microsoft.com/licensing/servicecenter/default.aspx

Applying your knowledge in the exam:

- You will almost certainly get a question or two on VLSC so remember the four main tasks that customers will use it for: managing and activating SA benefits, viewing consolidated license and agreement information, downloading software, and finding Volume License Keys

- Look out for the particular agreement that the customer has purchased licenses through – you should only recommend that they use VLSC when they have a Select Plus or Enterprise Agreement

Microsoft Volume Licensing Center (MVLC)

The Microsoft Volume Licensing Center (MVLC) is a brand new portal for customers who have bought licenses through an MPSA. You can broadly consider it as the replacement for VLSC in the sense that it offers the same sort of facilities such as viewing and managing SA benefits and downloading software and Volume Licensing Keys.

However, be aware that MVLC can ONLY be used to manage licenses acquired under the MPSA, so if a customer has existing licenses under another agreement then they will need to manage those through VLSC.

Since MVLC is a new tool you'd expect it to have some new features and indeed it does, the most important of which is the ability for customers to self-provision Online Services. This makes it quick and easy for them to access additional USLs to assign to users.

There is also a new tool for partners and this is called the Microsoft Volume Licensing Partner Center (MVLPC).

Applying your knowledge in the exam:

- Again, you will almost certainly get a question on MVLC so remember the FIVE main tasks that customers will use it for: managing SA benefits, viewing consolidated license and agreement information, downloading software, finding Volume License Keys, and self-provisioning Online Services

- Look out for the particular agreement that the customer has purchased licenses through – you should only recommend that they use MVLC when they have an MPSA

- If the customer has signed multiple agreements, one of which is an MPSA, remember that they will need to use both VLSC and MVLC to manage their licenses across the agreements

Product Activation

Product activation is technology that ensures that software is only installed on devices for which it is licensed. FPP and OEM software is activated with a Product Key which is either supplied with the media for the user to activate, or carried out by the System Builder. Software acquired through Volume Licensing agreements also needs to be activated with keys known as Volume License Keys or VLKs. You can imagine that if this had to be done manually for each individual machine it would be a time consuming task. So, technology known as Volume Activation (VA) automates the activation process. There have been changes and advances in the way this is achieved but, as usual, we'll focus on the way it was implemented at the time of the exam.

For Volume Licensing customers, the key products that need to be activated are Windows 8.1, Office 2013 and Windows Server 2012 R2. Volume Activation gives customers two alternatives to activate software: using a Multiple Activation Key (MAK) or the Key Management Service (KMS), and it's particularly these methods that you need to be familiar with for the exam.

KMS is the default method of activation and is suitable for customers who have more than 25 devices regularly connected to a network. This method activates the software on a device against a customer-hosted KMS server, and to remain activated, the device must renew the activation by connecting to this server at least once every 180 days.

Alternatively, MAK is recommended for organizations which have devices that rarely or never connect to the corporate network, or where the number of devices needing activation does not meet the KMS activation threshold of 25.

There are two types of MAK activation: independent and proxy. With independent activation, each device independently connects to and is activated by Microsoft servers. This can be done over the Internet or by telephone. The proxy activation enables a centralized activation request on behalf of multiple devices with a single connection to the Microsoft servers, and is useful for environments in which security restrictions do not allow all devices direct access to the Internet, for example.

For organizations that have a variety of devices, some of which do and some of which don't connect to the corporate network, it is possible to use a combination of activation methods.

Applying your knowledge in the exam:

- You may be asked to recommend a Volume Activation method for a particular customer, so look out for two key pieces of information – the number of PCs and whether they are regularly connected to a network. KMS is only an option if there are 25 or more devices, so recommend MAK if there is a specific group of less than 25 PCs that need to be activated. Then, if the devices aren't going to be regularly connected to a network it is better to do a one-off activation using MAK. Otherwise, of course, recommend KMS for devices that can be connected to the KMS server every 180 days

- Other acronyms may be used in the exam as suggested answers, such as Volume Activation (VA) and Volume License Key (VLK), and while these do exist as proper terms as we've seen, they are not specific types of activation, and therefore you shouldn't choose them as answers when asked to recommend how a Volume Licensing customer should activate their products

License Use Rights

As we mentioned earlier in the book, the use rights associated with a software license differ according to the channel that the license has been acquired through. Typically (and always for the exam), you would expect the use rights associated with FPP and OEM licenses to be more restrictive than those for licenses acquired through the Volume Licensing programs.

MSLT

FPP and OEM software is governed by the Microsoft Software License Terms which you can find at this link:
microsoft.com/en-us/legal/IntellectualProperty/UseTerms/Default.aspx

This site allows you to select a product, a version and a language, and will then generate a document containing Retail License Terms and OEM License Terms. This is extremely useful when you want to check the use rights for a particular product, or when a customer needs written confirmation of particular use rights.

Volume Licensing Product List

The Product List document is released monthly by Microsoft and gives further detail on the specifics of licensing products acquired through Volume Licensing programs. You can download it from:
www.microsoft.com/licensing/products/products.aspx

This document has a useful table for every single Microsoft Volume Licensing product where you can see the licensing programs that it's available through and the points allocations for the Select Plus and MPSA agreements. It also tells you the pool that the product falls into, the prior version, and in the case of subscription licenses, whether or not they're eligible to be reduced at anniversary.

There is also a comprehensive section on Software Assurance which explains which benefits are available through which programs and how the entitlements are calculated.

MPSA Licensing Manual

The MPSA Licensing Manual runs alongside the Product List covering information specific to the MPSA, and it can be found here: www.microsoftvolumelicensing.com/DocumentSearch.aspx

The most important thing to note about the MPSA Licensing Manual is that when you need to know about SA benefits and their calculation in the MPSA, this document should be used rather than the Product List. There are, however, reminders of this fact in the Product List should you forget!

Volume Licensing Product Use Rights (PUR)

Volume Licensing software use rights are documented in the Product Use Rights (PUR) document which is also available at: www.microsoft.com/licensing/products/products.aspx

The Product Use Rights document is released quarterly by Microsoft and details the product use rights of all software acquired through all Volume Licensing agreements. It contains information that explains the licensing terms that apply to all products, such as rights to use other versions of the software or when licenses may be reassigned, and then has sections for each of the different licensing models. Within the licensing models sections the information is broken down by product and it's where you would find, for example, information on whether Exchange Server has License Mobility rights, or the virtualization rights for the different editions of Windows Server.

Microsoft Online Services Terms (OST)

Consider this document to be the equivalent of the PUR for all of the online services and it's available at the same link: www.microsoft.com/licensing/products/products.aspx

This document is also released quarterly and again has some general terms that apply to all products and then there are sections for all of the individual online services. This is where you would see for example, which USLs give access to Exchange Online – apart from the obvious Plan 1 and Plan 2!

Applying your knowledge in the exam:

- You need to be able to select the right document from the choice above to recommend where customers should go to answer specific licensing questions. Make sure you get the easy questions right – if a customer needs to know the use rights for OEM or FPP software then the Microsoft Software License Terms is going to be the right recommendation. Equally, if you have a question about Online Services, then your first thought should be the OST document

- It's trickier to learn what's in the Product List and what's in the PUR. My recommendation would be to think of it like this: if it's a licensing fact (how many points is a SQL license under the MPSA?) then it's the Product List, whereas if it's about exercising a licensing right (how many virtual machines can I run under this license?) then it's the PUR

- If the customer has chosen the MPSA to purchase their licenses through then remember that if they need details about the SA benefits then they should refer to the MPSA Licensing Manual rather than the Product List

explore.ms

explore.ms is a web portal for Licensing Solution Providers (LSPs) and Distributors. It gives them access to agreement information for their customers as well as being a repository for agreements and forms, reports and other tools.

Applying your knowledge in the exam:

- Remember that explore.ms is a partner tool, so don't recommend it when you're asked where customers should go to manage their Volume Licensing agreements – when you should choose VLSC or MVLC of course

- You are more likely to see explore.ms as a suggested (wrong) answer in the exam, but knowing what it is means that you can disregard it as a possible answer with confidence

eAgreements

eAgreements is the tool which resellers and LSPs use to create a package of documents for customers signing new agreements. The documents can then be electronically signed by the customer and uploaded into the system, or processed as paper copies.

Applying your knowledge in the exam:

- Again, it is unlikely that you will be presented with a specific question on eAgreements, but it is likely to appear as a suggested answer, usually on a question about VLSC

Licensing Tools and Resources Revision Cards

Use the following one page summaries to review the key points about the licensing tools and product activation methods that you'll need to know for the exam.

Revision Card 37:

Volume Licensing Portals

Tool	Description
VLSC	Volume Licensing Service Center, used by Select Plus and Enterprise Agreement customers to: • manage and activate SA benefits • view consolidated license and agreement information • download software • find Volume License Keys
MVLC	Microsoft Volume Licensing Center, used by MPSA customers to: • manage SA benefits • view consolidated license and agreement information • download software • find Volume License Keys • self-provision Online Services

Revision Card 38:
Volume Licensing Activation Methods

Method	Key Points
KMS	Key Management Service: • Software activated against a customer-hosted KMS server • KMS activation threshold of 25 devices • Suitable for devices connected to a network • Activation renewed every 180 days
MAK	Multiple Activation Key: • Software activated against Microsoft servers • Independent activation: device connects directly to the activation server • Proxy activation: centralized activation request on behalf of multiple devices • One-time activation
Either method can be used to activate these products in Volume Licensing – WOW!	**W**indows 8.1 **O**ffice 2013 **W**indows Server 2012 R2

Revision Card 39:
Licensing Resources

Resource	Description
MSLT	The Microsoft Software License Terms detail the product use rights of OEM and FPP software
Product List	The Product List gives factual licensing information about each product
MPSA Licensing Manual	The MPSA Licensing Manual specifically supports the MPSA with SA benefit information
PUR	The Product Use Rights document details the product use rights of all on-premises software acquired through all Volume Licensing agreements
OST	The Online Services Terms document details the product use rights of Online Services acquired through all Volume Licensing agreements

Revision Card 40:
Licensing Tools

Tool	Description
explore.ms	A web portal for Licensing Solution Providers (LSPs) and Distributors which gives access to agreement information and other tools and resources
eAgreements	The tool which resellers and LSPs use to create a package of documents for customers signing new agreements

Recap Questions and Answers

Use these Recap Questions to see how much you know about the Microsoft licensing tools and resources. If you find any areas that you need to go over you can review the relevant topic in this section of the book. As usual, you'll find a couple of questions on each page with the answers when you turn over.

Questions 1 – 3

1. The Lemon Launderette have 275 PCs that regularly connect to their corporate network that they need to activate Office 2013 on. What method of activation would you recommend?
   a) VA 2.0
   b) VLK
   c) MAK
   d) KMS

2. Vermilion Jewellers have an existing Enterprise Agreement and have recently signed a Select Plus agreement for ad hoc purchases of licenses. Where should they go to manage the licenses acquired under these two agreements?
   a) eSelect for the Select Plus agreement and VLSC for the Enterprise Agreement
   b) VLSC for both agreements
   c) MVLS for both agreements
   d) explore.ms for the Select Plus agreement and MVLS for the Enterprise Agreement

3. The Software Asset Management team at Cerise Estate Management want to check on the use rights for the Office Professional Plus 2013 licenses that they have purchased through their Enterprise Agreement. Where should you refer them to?
   a) The Microsoft Software License Terms website
   b) The Volume Licensing Service Center
   c) The Product Use Rights document
   d) explore.ms

Answers 1 – 3

1. The Lemon Launderette have 275 PCs that regularly connect to their corporate network that they need to activate Office 2013 on. What method of activation would you recommend?

   a) VA 2.0
   b) VLK
   c) MAK
   d) **KMS** ✓

2. Vermilion Jewellers have an existing Enterprise Agreement and have recently signed a Select Plus agreement for ad hoc purchases of licenses. Where should they go to manage the licenses acquired under these two agreements?

   a) eSelect for the Select Plus agreement and VLSC for the Enterprise Agreement
   b) **VLSC for both agreements** ✓
   c) MVLS for both agreements
   d) explore.ms for the Select Plus agreement and MVLS for the Enterprise Agreement

3. The Software Asset Management team at Cerise Estate Management want to check on the use rights for the Office Professional Plus 2013 licenses that they have purchased through their Enterprise Agreement. Where should you refer them to?

   a) The Microsoft Software License Terms website
   b) The Volume Licensing Service Center
   c) **The Product Use Rights document** ✓
   d) explore.ms

Questions 4 – 7

4. The HR manager at Honeydew Hatters wants to see how many Training Vouchers her organization has allocated to them through their Enterprise Agreement. Where should she go to do this?

   a) Key Management Services (KMS)
   b) Software Assurance Benefits Portal (SABP)
   c) Volume Licensing Service Center (VLSC)
   d) Microsoft Volume Licensing Center (MVLC)

5. The IT manager at The Papaya Hire Company is ready to deploy Windows 8.1 Enterprise. Where should he go to download the software?

   a) Software Assurance Benefits Portal (SABP)
   b) Volume Licensing Service Center (VLSC)
   c) The Microsoft Downloads site
   d) explore.ms

6. Taupe Telecoms have deployed Office Professional Plus 2013 and are ready to activate it. Where should they get the Volume License Keys from?

   a) Volume Licensing Service Center (VLSC)
   b) The Microsoft Downloads site
   c) explore.ms
   d) Microsoft VLK Center

7. Mauve Stoves have signed an MPSA with SAM for the Servers pool. Where should the IT Training Manager go to allocate some Training Vouchers?

   a) Volume Licensing Service Center (VLSC)
   b) Microsoft Volume Licensing Center (MVLC)
   c) Software Assurance Benefits Portal (SABP)
   d) Microsoft Volume Licensing Purchasing Center (MVLPC)

4. The HR manager at Honeydew Hatters wants to see how many Training Vouchers her organization has allocated to them through their Enterprise Agreement. Where should she go to do this?

   a) Key Management Services (KMS)
   b) Software Assurance Benefits Portal (SABP)
   c) Volume Licensing Service Center (VLSC) ✓
   d) Microsoft Volume Licensing Center (MVLC)

5. The IT manager at The Papaya Hire Company is ready to deploy Windows 8.1 Enterprise. Where should he go to download the software?

   a) Software Assurance Benefits Portal (SABP)
   b) Volume Licensing Service Center (VLSC) ✓
   c) The Microsoft Downloads site
   d) explore.ms

6. Taupe Telecoms have deployed Office Professional Plus 2013 and are ready to activate it. Where should they get the Volume License Keys from?

   a) Volume Licensing Service Center (VLSC) ✓
   b) The Microsoft Downloads site
   c) explore.ms
   d) Microsoft VLK Center

7. Mauve Stoves have signed an MPSA with SAM for the Servers pool. Where should the IT Training Manager go to allocate some Training Vouchers?

   a) Volume Licensing Service Center (VLSC)
   b) Microsoft Volume Licensing Center (MVLC) ✓
   c) Software Assurance Benefits Portal (SABP)
   d) Microsoft Volume Licensing Purchasing Center (MVLPC)

Questions 8 – 11

8. Purple Paint Pot Decorators have bought Windows and Office software pre-installed on their new laptops. Where should they go to check the license terms associated with this software?
   a) The Microsoft Software License Terms website
   b) The Volume Licensing Service Center
   c) The Product Use Rights document
   d) explore.ms

9. Which of the following tasks can customers perform through the MVLC? Choose three answers.
   a) Self-provision Online Services
   b) Download software
   c) Manage Software Assurance benefits
   d) Order licenses for on-premises software
   e) View consolidated licensing information across any agreements

10. The procurement manager at Cyan Ida's Pharmacy would like to be sure that her Office 365 E3 USLs purchased through the MPSA give access to SharePoint Online. Where should she go to confirm this?
    a) The PUR
    b) The OST
    c) The Product List
    d) The MPSA Licensing Manual

11. The IT manager at Xanthic Tractors would like to know how the 24x7 Problem Resolution Support allocation is calculated for his MPSA. Where should he go to find these calculations?
    a) The PUR
    b) The OST
    c) The Product List
    d) The MPSA Licensing Manual

8. Purple Paint Pot Decorators have bought Windows and Office software pre-installed on their new laptops. Where should they go to check the license terms associated with this software?

    a) **The Microsoft Software License Terms website** ✓
    b) The Volume Licensing Service Center
    c) The Product Use Rights document
    d) explore.ms

9. Which of the following tasks can customers perform through the MVLC? Choose three answers.

    a) **Self-provision Online Services** ✓
    b) **Download software** ✓
    c) **Manage Software Assurance benefits** ✓
    d) Order licenses for on-premises software
    e) View consolidated licensing information across any agreements

10. The procurement manager at Cyan Ida's Pharmacy would like to be sure that her Office 365 E3 USLs purchased through the MPSA give access to SharePoint Online. Where should she go to confirm this?

    a) The PUR
    b) **The OST** ✓
    c) The Product List
    d) The MPSA Licensing Manual

11. The IT manager at Xanthic Tractors would like to know how the 24x7 Problem Resolution Support allocation is calculated for his MPSA. Where should he go to find these calculations?

    a) The PUR
    b) The OST
    c) The Product List
    d) **The MPSA Licensing Manual** ✓

Questions 12 – 14

12. Peach Snaps Cameras have purchased Office Professional Plus 2013 for ten laptops. These laptops are standalone devices in their test lab and are not connected to the Internet. How would you recommend that they activate Office 2013?
    a) MAK proxy activation
    b) VLK
    c) MAK independent activation
    d) KMS

13. Ochre Poker have an existing Enterprise Agreement and have recently signed an MPSA for ad hoc purchases of licenses. Where should they go to manage the licenses acquired under these two agreements?
    a) MVLC for the MPSA and VLSC for the Enterprise Agreement
    b) VLSC for both agreements
    c) MVLC for both agreements
    d) VLSC for the MPSA and MVLC for the Enterprise Agreement

14. The IT manager at Tangerine Truckers has gone to VLSC to download SQL Server 2005 Datacenter edition but cannot find it in the list of software. Why is this?
    a) He has purchased software through MPSA so cannot download software through VLSC
    b) If he has not purchased a license for the product it will not be available to download in VLSC
    c) There was no Datacenter edition for SQL Server 2005
    d) Only software of the current or immediately prior version is available for download in VLSC

12. Peach Snaps Cameras have purchased Office Professional Plus 2013 for ten laptops. These laptops are standalone devices in their test lab and are not connected to the Internet. How would you recommend that they activate Office 2013?

    a) **MAK proxy activation** ✓
    b) VLK
    c) MAK independent activation
    d) KMS

13. Ochre Poker have an existing Enterprise Agreement and have recently signed an MPSA for ad hoc purchases of licenses. Where should they go to manage the licenses acquired under these two agreements?

    a) **MVLC for the MPSA and VLSC for the Enterprise Agreement** ✓
    b) VLSC for both agreements
    c) MVLC for both agreements
    d) VLSC for the MPSA and MVLC for the Enterprise Agreement

14. The IT manager at Tangerine Truckers has gone to VLSC to download SQL Server 2005 Datacenter edition but cannot find it in the list of software. Why is this?

    a) He has purchased software through MPSA so cannot download software through VLSC
    b) If he has not purchased a license for the product it will not be available to download in VLSC
    c) There was no Datacenter edition for SQL Server 2005
    d) **Only software of the current or immediately prior version is available for download in VLSC** ✓

Questions 15 – 17

15. The IT manager at Turquoise Toys cannot remember how many virtual machines he may run Windows Server in when he assigns a single license to a two-processor server. Where should he go to confirm this?
    a) The PUR
    b) The OST
    c) The Product List
    d) eAgreements

16. The procurement manager at Mellow Yellow Sounds is aware that his annual points check is approaching for his MPSA and he is not sure he will meet the 500 points minimum without further purchases. Where should he go to check the points allocations of products he is interested in buying?
    a) The PUR
    b) The OST
    c) The Product List
    d) The MPSA Licensing Manual

17. Which of the following products need to be activated? Choose three answers.
    a) Windows 8.1
    b) Windows Server 2012 R2
    c) System Center 2012 R2
    d) SQL Server 2014
    e) Office 2013
    f) Project Server 2013

15. The IT manager at Turquoise Toys cannot remember how many virtual machines he may run Windows Server in when he assigns a single license to a two-processor server. Where should he go to confirm this?
    a) **The PUR** ✓
    b) The OST
    c) The Product List
    d) eAgreements

16. The procurement manager at Mellow Yellow Sounds is aware that his annual points check is approaching for his MPSA and he is not sure he will meet the 500 points minimum without further purchases. Where should he go to check the points allocations of products he is interested in buying?
    a) The PUR
    b) The OST
    c) **The Product List** ✓
    d) The MPSA Licensing Manual

17. Which of the following products need to be activated? Choose three answers.
    a) **Windows 8.1** ✓
    b) **Windows Server 2012 R2** ✓
    c) System Center 2012 R2
    d) SQL Server 2014
    e) **Office 2013** ✓
    f) Project Server 2013

PART 6: FINAL PREPARATIONS FOR THE EXAM

The Exam Syllabus

There are four key areas covered in the exam. Let's take a look at these areas to explore in a little more detail what they mean and which sections of the book will help you with the knowledge that you'll need.

Recommend the Appropriate Technology Solution (30-35%)

Questions relating to this area will require you to determine the right on-premises or Online Services product to meet a customer's needs, and then to identify the appropriate product licensing rights and apply them to the customer requirements. Use "Part 2: The Microsoft Products and Their Licensing Models" and "Part 5: Licensing Tools and Resources" for the information that you'll need to answer questions in this area.

Recommend the Appropriate Software Assurance Benefits (15-20%)

Questions relating to this area will require you to identify SA benefits that match a particular customer need. You'll find the information that you need for this area in "Part 4: Software Assurance".

Recommend a Licensing Solution (30-35%)

Questions relating to this area will require you to work out the best way for the customer to acquire the licenses that they need. First of all, you'll have to choose between FPP, OEM and Volume Licensing and then, where appropriate, recommend a particular Volume Licensing program. "Part 3: The Microsoft Licensing Agreements" contains the information that you'll need to answer questions in this area.

Provide Post-Sales Customer Service (10-15%)

Questions relating to this area will cover topics such as helping customers to activate their software, download the products that they need, as well as managing and activating their SA benefits. The information that you'll need for questions in this area is all contained in "Part 5: Licensing Tools and Resources".

The Exam Structure

As I mentioned right at the beginning of this book, the exam will contain a customer scenario on which you will have to answer around 10 questions, and then there will be a whole series of about 50 individual questions which could be on any aspect of Microsoft licensing.

The Exam Scenario

The information that you'll be given in the scenario will be split into a number of sections. First of all, there will be an Overview section where you'll be told details such as the name of the company, where it's located, how long it's operated for, and how many employees there are. Then there will be a section on the Existing Environment and this will contain information on the current IT infrastructure and how the company purchases its existing licenses. You may find some problem statements in this section too. And finally there is a Requirements section where the future plans for the company are documented which, again, are typically either IT infrastructure related or are to do with improving license acquisition and management.

The questions that follow will ask you to recommend products, licensing models, SA benefits, the programs through which the customer should be acquiring the required licenses, and the relevant licensing tools. One thing to note is that the questions you're given are randomized – there could be a bank of 20 questions for the scenario and you'll be given up to about ten of them to answer. This does mean that the questions themselves are completely independent of each other within a single scenario. So, if you've decided that a Select Plus agreement is the way to go in question 1, but the answer to question 3 is clearly an Enterprise Subscription Agreement, don't doubt your answer to question 1 – the questions are completely separate!

Time-wise, you should aim to spend around 30 minutes in tackling the reading of the scenario and answering the questions. You'll have the opportunity to review, check and change any answers that you want to, and then you need to commit by submitting the scenario. At that point you'll move on to the general licensing questions section.

Question Types

There are several different question types in the exam which you'll come across both in the scenario and in the general questions section, and so in this part of the book I've mocked up some sample questions to give you an idea of what to expect. And, as usual, these are not actual questions from the exam but straight out of my head.

Multiple Choice

Most of the questions will be multiple choice and you'll always be told how many answers to select if there are multiple parts to the answer.

Underlined Text

In this type of question you'll be given a statement with some underlined text in it and you need to decide if it's correct or not. If it is indeed correct, then you need to choose the "No change needed" option, otherwise you need to choose the option that would replace the underlined text to make the statement correct:

> Under the MPSA, several Affiliates may purchase under the same agreement to benefit from consolidated price levels.
>
> To answer, choose the option "No change needed" if the underlined text is correct. If the underlined text is not correct, choose the correct answer.
>
> A   ◯ Departments
>
> B   ◯ Purchasing Accounts
>
> C   ◯ No change needed
>
> D   ◯ Companies

Figure 39: Underlined Text Question

In this example, the question is referring to Purchasing Accounts so you should choose that answer.

Multiple Yes/No Options

The Multiple Yes/No questions give you a series of statements on the same topic and you need to evaluate whether each of them is true by choosing Yes or No. In this example, all of the statements are about the CAL Suites:

For each of the following statements, select Yes if the statement is true. Otherwise, select No.

	Yes	No
The Enterprise CAL Suite includes approximately 12 CALs including a SQL CAL	○	○
The Core CAL Suite and Enterprise CAL Suite may be licensed by User or by Device	○	○
Customers may step-up from the Core CAL Suite to the Enterprise CAL Suite	○	○

Figure 40: Multiple Yes/No Options Question

You should choose No for the first statement, and then Yes for the other two. Note that if there are several statements, then you may need to scroll down in the box.

Multiple Select

In the Multiple Select questions you need to compare two or more items by selecting attributes. In this example you can see that we're comparing a Select Plus and an Enterprise Agreement and you'd need to check the boxes if the items on the left hand side applied to the agreements:

A customer is interested in how the Select Plus and Enterprise Agreements compare and you need to highlight the differences. To answer, select the appropriate features for each agreement in the answer area.

	Select Plus	Enterprise Agreement
3 year term	☐	☐
Software Assurance optional	☐	☐
Can buy Online Services	☐	☐
Can buy on-premises software	☐	☐

Figure 41: Multiple Select Question

Remember that because these are check boxes you can check some, all or none of the options, unlike the Multiple Yes/No Options above when you have to select one, and only one, option per line.

To score full marks on this question you would select the first option for the EA only, the second for Select Plus only, the third for the EA only, and the final option for both agreements.

Drop Down Options

The Drop Down Options questions require you to choose the correct answer from a drop down box. In this example, you have to choose how many Windows Server 2012 R2 Standard licenses you would need to license each of the scenarios detailed on the left hand side:

How many Windows Server 2012 R2 Standard licenses are required to license the machines detailed below? To answer, choose the number of licenses required in the answer area.

Scenario	Licenses Required
4 processors, 4 VMs	Select... ▾
2 processors, 6 VMs	Select... ▾
8 processors, 3 VMs	Select... ▾

Figure 42: Drop Down Options Question

You should choose 2, 3, and 4 to score full marks. Note that you could be given multiple drop down options and if you want to choose 0 from the list then you need to actively select it – it won't be the default option.

Drag and Drop

The Drag and Drop questions give you a list of choices on the left hand side which you need to match to the items on the right hand side. In this example, you need to choose the correct licensing model for each of the products listed and you would do this by dragging the relevant licensing model to the boxes next to the products:

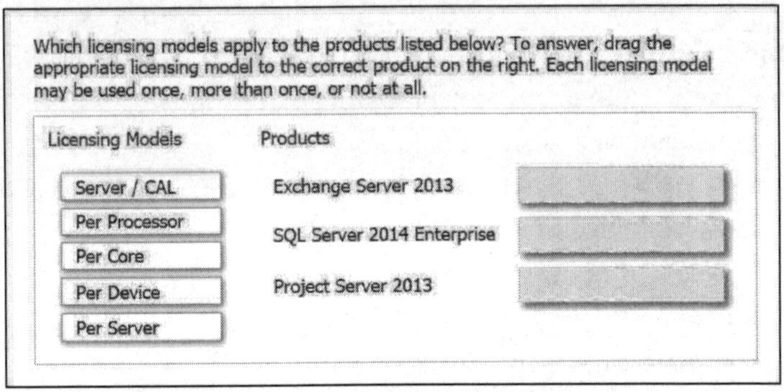

Which licensing models apply to the products listed below? To answer, drag the appropriate licensing model to the correct product on the right. Each licensing model may be used once, more than once, or not at all.

Licensing Models	Products
Server / CAL	Exchange Server 2013
Per Processor	SQL Server 2014 Enterprise
Per Core	
Per Device	Project Server 2013
Per Server	

Figure 43: Drag and Drop Question

Here you would drag "Server / CAL" to the box next to Exchange Server 2013 and "Per Core" next to SQL Server 2014 Enterprise. You would then drag "Server / CAL" next to Project Server 2013 as well since you are allowed to drag an option multiple times to the right hand boxes if required.

Ordering

In the Ordering questions you need to drag options on the left to boxes on the right ensuring that a process is in the correct order. In this example, you have to choose three items and put them in the right order to show how the process for a customer being able to purchase under an MPSA works:

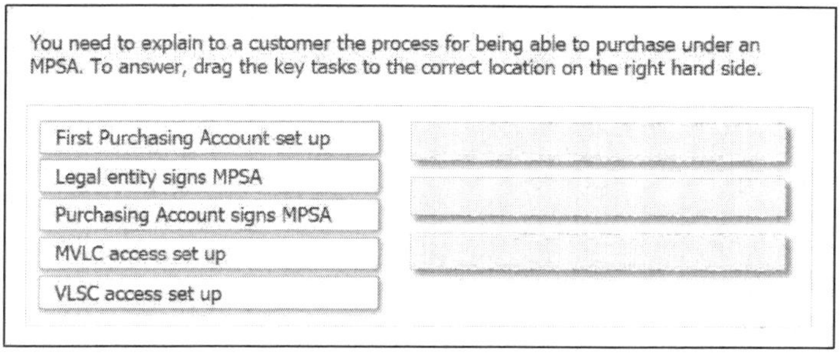

You need to explain to a customer the process for being able to purchase under an MPSA. To answer, drag the key tasks to the correct location on the right hand side.

First Purchasing Account set up

Legal entity signs MPSA

Purchasing Account signs MPSA

MVLC access set up

VLSC access set up

Figure 44: Ordering Question

Here you should drag "Legal entity signs MPSA", followed by "First Purchasing Account set up", followed by "MVLC access set up".

Exam Hints

One of the most helpful hints I can give you for the exam is not to over-complicate things. When you're reading the questions don't look for hidden agenda or meaning that will make the question significantly more difficult to answer. Don't delve too deeply from a technical perspective either – if a company wants to deploy a network infrastructure, then the answer will be to deploy Windows Server. Don't worry that you might have read something in the business goals or current infrastructure that would make this technically impossible, for example.

And finally, there are no marks deducted for wrong answers so you should absolutely answer every question in the exam. When you just don't know the right answer you should, of course, take a guess, but make sure it's a calculated one – eliminate any suggested answers that you know are wrong and then choose from the answers that are left.

The Language of the Exam

One of the things that people find hardest about taking the exam is not the licensing knowledge, or learning about the programs and SA benefits, it's interpreting the questions and working out what the intent of the question is. Use the "applying your knowledge in the exam" points in the main sections so that you're comfortable with the sorts of things you need to look out for.

Your Final Preparations

Make sure that you're completely comfortable with the four key areas that make up Parts 2 to 5 of this book; use the Revision Cards and learn all of the facts as well as you can.

Finally, put all your knowledge into practice and work through the sample scenario that you'll find in the next section.

And when the exam is all over, email us at info@licensingschool.co.uk to let us know you've passed – we're always interested!

PART 7: SAMPLE SCENARIO

This scenario is designed to give you a feel for the scenario that you'll be presented with in the exam. It is not the actual exam scenario re-worded, it's simply in the same style and is genuinely made up out of my head! So, don't learn the answers, just use it to get into the mind-set of the exam and to see if you still have gaps in your knowledge.

My advice would be to read the scenario through completely and then to tackle the questions. The answers are then given on the following pages along with an explanation as to why a particular answer is correct. I've given you 12 questions to tackle and this will be similar to what you'll find in the real exam.

Sample Exam Scenario: Fandango Fitness

Company Background

- Fandango Fitness are headquartered in the UK with 1,500 staff working in fitness centers all over the country. They own five subsidiary companies located in the US, Australia and mainland Europe to carry out local operations in those geographies

- The business started ten years ago and has grown steadily. Although the management team have adopted a cautious approach to growing the company, they feel they are now ready for a more aggressive expansion and envisage doubling the turnover of the business in the next two years

Existing Environment

- Fandango Fitness have an expiring Select Plus agreement through which they have purchased perpetual licenses for their 1,250 PCs. All of the subsidiary companies have used their own Open agreements or OEM software to license the devices and servers that they use. There are 480 PCs in total across these organizations. All PCs are running a variety of editions and versions of Windows, ranging from Windows XP Professional on the majority of machines to Windows 7 Professional on a few devices

- All of the PCs in the head office (150) are licensed for Microsoft Office Professional Plus 2013 through the Select Plus agreement. 75 of these PCs are due for retirement and will be replaced by state-of-the-art laptops

- All organizations are running a client-server network running Windows Server 2008 Enterprise, and access to the servers is licensed with Windows Server 2008 Device CALs

- Email and basic intranet sites are provided by Exchange Server 2010 and SharePoint Server 2010

Business Goals

- The senior management team at Fandango Fitness would like to consolidate the various existing licensing agreements that have been signed across the main organization and its subsidiaries. Their goal would be to use a single agreement if this were possible, but they need reassurance as they are worried about the upfront costs of moving to any new agreement

- The IT department have put forward a proposal which shows the benefits of standardizing the desktop across the entire organization including subsidiaries. They propose always using the latest versions of the desktop software and to roll out a single image with the capability for users to choose which language they wish to work in

- They would like to upgrade their entire server infrastructure and start using Unified Messaging capabilities throughout the wider organization. Their goal is to keep the whole infrastructure current once it has been upgraded. They will move to a virtualized environment where they will run approximately 20 virtual machines on each server at any one time, with the intention of extending the server farm to Azure within 12 months

- Fandango Fitness plan to initiate a number of global projects which will require that employees from all offices are in regular communication with each other and able to share documents, presentations and spreadsheets easily. They are worried, however, about the cost of phone calls spiraling out of control and would like to be able to control this

- Fandango Fitness would like to enable users to work at home on the same software that they use in the office. Employees will also need to access SharePoint sites and use their corporate email from home

- Fandango Fitness will start to use self-employed fitness instructors at their centers and will give them basic email capability and access to the company intranet through Microsoft Online Services

Questions

1. You need to recommend a way for Fandango Fitness to purchase their licenses to meet their business goal of agreement consolidation. What would you recommend?

   a) An Enterprise Agreement for Fandango Fitness and a Select Plus agreement for the affiliates
   b) A single Enterprise Agreement for all organizations
   c) A single MPSA agreement for all organizations
   d) An Enterprise Subscription Agreement for Fandango Fitness and an MPSA agreement for the affiliates

2. You decide to recommend an Enterprise Agreement for Fandango Fitness and its affiliates. What price level will they be entitled to?

   a) Level A
   b) Level B
   c) Level C
   d) Level D

3. How would you recommend that Fandango Fitness license the fitness instructors in the most cost-effective way?

   a) Exchange Server 2013 Standard CALs
   b) Exchange Online Plan 1
   c) Office 365 Plan E1
   d) Office 365 Plan K1

4. Fandango Fitness sign an Enterprise Agreement to make license purchases for their upcoming projects. Where should the procurement team go to get a single view of all of the licenses that have been purchased as the projects progress?

   a) Microsoft Volume Licensing Center
   b) eAgreements
   c) Volume Licensing Service Center
   d) LicenseView

5. Fandango Fitness decide to purchase SA on all their desktop licenses. Why is this important for them when you consider their business goals? Choose two answers.

   a) They need to be able to purchase Step Up licenses
   b) They always want to use the latest versions of the software
   c) They want users to use the same software at home as at work through the Home Use Program
   d) They intend to refresh much of their hardware

6. What licenses will Fandango Fitness need to order for the Unified Messaging solution that they want to deploy? Choose three answers.

   a) Exchange Server 2013 Server license
   b) Exchange Server 2013 External Connector license
   c) Exchange Server 2013 Standard CALs
   d) Exchange Server 2013 Enterprise CALs
   e) Exchange Server 2013 Voice CALs

7. What type of CALs should Fandango Fitness and their affiliates buy?

   a) Device CALs since there are more users than devices and this will save them money
   b) User CALs since they want people to be able to work from home and access corporate resources from there
   c) User CALs since there are less users than devices and this will save them money
   d) Device CALs since they are refreshing hardware and can re-use these CALs

8. Which of the following SA benefits will meet the business goals of the IT department? Choose two answers.

   a) License Mobility through Software Assurance
   b) Unlimited Virtualization Rights
   c) License Mobility within Server Farms
   d) Roaming Use Rights

9. How would you recommend that Fandango Fitness license their new replacement head office laptops with Office Professional Plus 2013?

    a) They should buy Office Professional 2013 pre-installed
    b) They should start a new Open agreement to purchase these licenses
    c) They should wait to purchase these licenses until the new agreement structure is in place
    d) They should reassign licenses from PCs that are being retired

10. What product would you recommend to help Fandango Fitness stop the costs of employee to employee phone calls rising as the need for collaboration increases?

    a) Exchange Server 2013
    b) Office Communications Server 2013
    c) SharePoint Server 2013
    d) Lync Server 2013

11. As Fandango Fitness start to consider consolidating all of their licenses, they want to check the use rights of licenses acquired through the expiring Open and Select Plus agreements. What would you recommend that they use?

    a) The Volume Licensing Service Center
    b) The Product Use Rights document
    c) The Microsoft Software License Terms website
    d) The Product List document

12. Fandango Fitness will manage their new server farm with System Center 2012 R2. What licenses would you recommend that they acquire to license the core infrastructure of the updated server farm?

    a) Windows Server 2012 R2 Datacenter + System Center 2012 R2 Datacenter licenses
    b) Windows Server 2012 R2 Standard + System Center 2012 R2 Standard licenses
    c) Core Infrastructure Server Suite Standard licenses
    d) Core Infrastructure Server Suite Datacenter licenses

Answers with Explanations

1. You need to recommend a way for Fandango Fitness to purchase their licenses to meet their business goal of agreement consolidation. What would you recommend?

   - Answer: A single Enterprise Agreement for all organizations
   - Reason: The subsidiary organizations meet the requirements to be affiliates under a single Enterprise Agreement for Fandango Fitness, since all subsidiaries are completely owned. They want to standardize the desktop across all organizations and upgrade the server infrastructure which everyone will access, making a Platform EA attractive

2. You decide to recommend an Enterprise Agreement for Fandango Fitness and its affiliates. What price level will they be entitled to?

   - Answer: Level A
   - Reason: There are 1,730 PCs in total which falls into the Level A band of between 250 and 2,400 PCs

3. How would you recommend that Fandango Fitness license the fitness instructors in the most cost-effective way?

   - Answer: Office 365 Plan K1
   - Reason: We are told that the fitness instructors will need basic email capability and access to the company intranet through Microsoft Online Services which indicates Exchange Online and SharePoint Online. The Exchange CALs and Plan 1 don't include SharePoint, and of the remaining options, the K1 Plan is the most cost-effective

4. Fandango Fitness sign an Enterprise Agreement to make license purchases for their upcoming projects. Where should the procurement team go to get a single view of all of the licenses that have been purchased as the projects progress?

   - Answer: Volume Licensing Service Center
   - Reason: VLSC is the tool that EA customers should use to get access to this information. Note that LicenseView is a fictional tool

5. Fandango Fitness decide to purchase SA on all their desktop licenses. Why is this important for them when you consider their business goals? Choose two answers.

   - Answer: They always want to use the latest versions of the software
   - Answer: They want users to use the same software at home as at work through the Home Use Program
   - Reason: Although the ability to purchase Step Up licenses is an SA benefit, there is no particular business goal stated that makes this benefit attractive to Fandango Fitness. Equally, although they do intend to refresh some of their hardware, this does not map to a specific SA benefit. The other two answers are both valid SA benefits and map to stated requirements of Fandango Fitness

6. What licenses will Fandango Fitness need to order for the Unified Messaging solution that they want to deploy? Choose three answers.

   - Answer: Exchange Server 2013 Server license
   - Answer: Exchange Server 2013 Standard CALs
   - Answer: Exchange Server 2013 Enterprise CALs
   - Reason: Exchange Server delivers the Unified Messaging solution (hence the Server license) and since it's the enterprise functionality of this product, users or devices should be licensed with Standard AND Enterprise CALs. Note that the Voice CAL is a fictional CAL

7. What type of CALs should Fandango Fitness and their affiliates buy?
   - Answer: User CALs since they want people to be able to work from home and access corporate resources from there
   - Reason: We are not specifically told the total number of users across the organizations and so the cost-saving answers can be dismissed. Although 75 PCs are being replaced by laptops this won't drive the need for a particular CAL. However, one of the business goals is to allow people to work from home, and licensing users with User CALs will mean that they are licensed to work both in the office and at home

8. Which of the following SA benefits will meet the business goals of the IT department? Choose two answers.
   - Answer: License Mobility through Software Assurance
   - Answer: License Mobility within Server Farms
   - Reason: All of the choices are valid SA benefits, however there is no stated business goal that would lead to a requirement for Unlimited Virtualization Rights or Roaming Use Rights. They are virtualizing the server farm where there will be up to 20 virtual machines on a physical server at any one time – indicating that virtual machines will move between servers, and so will need License Mobility within Server Farms. Also, they will extend the server farm to Azure which requires License Mobility through SA

9. How would you recommend that Fandango Fitness license their new replacement head office laptops with Office Professional Plus 2013?
   - Answer: They should reassign licenses from PCs that are being retired
   - Reason: One of the benefits of buying licenses through a Volume Licensing agreement is being able to reassign licenses and since there are PCs that are being retired this is an ideal opportunity to reassign and thus re-use the licenses. Note this answer is completely independent of other answers relating to an EA

10. What product would you recommend to help Fandango Fitness stop the costs of employee to employee phone calls rising as the need for collaboration increases?

- Answer: Lync Server 2013
- Reason: Fandango Fitness will be able to make use of the Lync Server enterprise telephony features to keep the cost of phone calls down

11. As Fandango Fitness start to consider consolidating all of their licenses, they want to check the use rights of licenses acquired through the expiring Open and Select Plus agreements. What would you recommend that they use?

- Answer: The Product Use Rights document
- Reason: Use rights for all licenses acquired through a Volume Licensing program are documented in the Product Use Rights document

12. Fandango Fitness will manage their new server farm with System Center 2012 R2. What licenses would you recommend that they acquire to license the core infrastructure of the updated server farm?

- Answer: Core Infrastructure Server Suite Datacenter licenses
- Reason: We are told that they will be updating their entire server infrastructure which will include Windows Server. Extra information in the question indicates that System Center needs to be acquired as well, and the most cost-effective way of acquiring licenses for these two products is to purchase Core Infrastructure Server Suite licenses. We are also told that there will be up to 20 virtual machines running on a server which would lead to a recommendation of the Datacenter edition since this is more cost-effective for higher levels of virtualization

Acknowledgements

Thanks to Simon Taylor for proof reading with the beadiest eyes in the business; if there are still errors then the fault is mine as I had the final say. Thanks also to Simon for coming up with all the fictional company names that are used throughout.

Thanks to Simona Millham, the creative brain behind the graphics used in this book. Again, if any are less than perfect it's due to my tweaking.

A special thank you to Paul Burgum, a business partner in a million, without whose guidance, support, and endless supply of good ideas I would not have been able to put this book together.

Louise Ulrick